A GLOSSARY OF THE
EUROPEAN UNION

Politics Glossaries

Series Editor: Keith Faulks

This series introduces key terms within the core subject areas of politics. The aim is to provide a brief, clear and convenient A–Z guide to the central concepts of the various branches of politics.

The series provides thorough, authoritative and concise reference works which offer clear and consistent coverage of both traditional and contemporary terminology. Students and teachers of politics at all levels of study will find the books invaluable, though the books are aimed primarily at readers new to a subject area. In addition to appealing to mainstream politics students, the series will also appeal to those studying courses in sociology, journalism, media studies and social policy that include elements of politics.

Volumes in the series provide:

- Dedicated coverage of particular topics within politics
- Coverage of key terms and major figures
- Practical examples of the terms defined
- Cross-references to related terms

Titles in the series include:

John Hoffman, *A Glossary of Political Theory*
Alistair Jones, *A Glossary of the European Union*
Alex Thomson, *A Glossary of US Politics and Government*
Duncan Watts, *A Glossary of UK Government and Politics*

A Glossary of the European Union

Alistair Jones

Edinburgh University Press

© Alistair Jones, 2008

Edinburgh University Press Ltd
22 George Square, Edinburgh

Typeset in 10.5/13 Sabon by
Servis Filmsetting Ltd, Manchester, and
printed and bound in Great Britain by
Antony Rowe Ltd, Chippenham, Wilts

A CIP record for this book is
available from the British Library

ISBN 978 0 7486 2575 8 (hardback)
ISBN 978 0 7486 2576 5 (paperback)

Contents

Tables

Acknowledgements

Many people need to be acknowledged for their assistance in the writing of this Glossary. First, as ever, is my wife Claire. Without her support and encouragement, the task of writing the Glossary would have taken even longer than it did.

Colleagues at De Montfort University should also be mentioned for their support. I thank all my colleagues in the Department of Public Policy, and especially Clive Gray, Tony Stott and John Greenwood. From elsewhere in the University, I thank Alison Statham, Nicky Drucquer and David Wilson.

I would like to thank the series editor, Keith Faulks, for his support and encouragement. From Edinburgh University Press, I wish to thank the staff involved there for their support. In particular, special acknowledgement should be made of Nicola Ramsey.

As ever, I wish to thank all of our pets: Nua (who sadly died while the Glossary was being written), Sasha, Max and Tiny. Their constant demands for attention, food, walks, or any other distractions that they could use gave many an opportunity for me to take a break from writing.

Finally, I take responsibility for any errors in or omissions from the Glossary. I hope that all users find it of some help.

Alistair Jones
April 2007

Introduction

As an undergraduate student some time last century, I remember grappling with a number of terms linked to the European Union (EU). These included words such as neo-functionalism, integration and supranationalism (to name but three). At that time, there was no resource to give brief explanations of such terms. Surprisingly, little has changed today. When people discuss issues surrounding the EU, they come into contact with terms which are unfamiliar to them. Concepts such as 'subsidiarity' or the 'emergency brake' may trip off the tongues of experts, but to the student or lay person they may as well be a foreign language.

The aim of this text is not only to explain these terms, but also to explain them in a straightforward manner. By making these terms accessible to students, there is then potential for a greater understanding of the EU to develop. A greater understanding of the organisation should not be equated with greater support for it. One of the best-informed politicians in the United Kingdom on the issue of the EU was Sir Teddy Taylor – a profound eurosceptic who resigned as a junior minister in the 1970s when Edward Heath applied for membership of the European Economic Community!

What is also important to realise is that many of the terms are interlinked. This Glossary highlights the way in which the terms are interlinked by emboldening key concepts. Thus, when examining the definition of neo-functionalism, for example, other key concepts that are explained in the

Glossary are highlighted. Other terms utilised in the definition will be presented as follows: **integration**. Any terms that are emboldened in such a manner contain their own separate explanation elsewhere in the Glossary. Other related terms may also be listed at the bottom of the explanation. Again, these terms will be emboldened.

It is not only key terms that are explained in the Glossary. Potted biographies of prominent individuals are also presented. The list includes Jean Monnet, Margaret Thatcher and Jacques Delors. Their biographies focus upon their role within the development of the European Union. The actions of individuals that are unrelated to the EU are excluded.

The Glossary is presented in alphabetical order. The prominent individuals are included by their surname. For example, the founding father of the EU is listed as **Monnet, Jean**.

For some terms, suggestions for further reading are also included. These are to provide extra resources to build upon the introduction to the terms provided in this Glossary.

The intention of this Glossary is not for the student or lay person to read it from cover to cover. Not even the most enthused europhile would wish to inflict such torture upon people. Rather, it is here to supplement reading that is carried out elsewhere; to provide explanations of difficult concepts to enable people to better understand what they are reading on the subject of the European Union.

A Glossary of the
European Union

A

ACP countries   see **African, Caribbean and Pacific (ACP) countries**

acquis communautaire   The **European Union** legislation that must be taken on board by any **state** joining the organisation. It includes policies as well as legislation. In theory, any applicant state must adopt the entire *acquis*. It may, however, be possible for an applicant to negotiate over specific policies. At the end of the negotiations, the applicant state must accept the *acquis*. Currently there are 31 chapters to the *acquis communautaire*. These are detailed in Table A1.

Table A1   The 31 chapters of the *acquis communautaire*

1. Free movement of goods	18. Education and training
2. Freedom of movement for persons	19. Telecommunications and information technologies
3. Freedom to provide services	20. Cultural and audio-visual policy
4. Free movement of capital	21. Regional policy and co-ordination of social structures
5. Company law	
6. Competition policy	22. Environment
7. Agriculture	23. Consumers and health protection
8. Fisheries	
9. Transport policy	24. Co-operation in the fields of justice and home affairs
10. Taxation	
11. Economic and monetary union	25. Customs union
	26. External relations
12. Statistics	27. Common foreign and security policy
13. Social policy and employment	
	28. Financial control
14. Energy	29. Financial and budgetary provisions
15. Industrial policy	
16. Small and medium-sized enterprises	30. Institutions
17. Science and research	31. Other

Adenauer, Konrad (1876–1967) Adenauer was the first chancellor of West Germany (from 1949 to 1963). It was he who successfully negotiated West German membership of the **European Coal and Steel Community** in the late 1940s and early 1950s. Adenauer has been credited with the rehabilitation of West Germany back into the international fold, after being ostracised in the aftermath of the Second World War. This was done by developing strong ties with both the French (via the Coal and Steel Community) and the Americans (via support for the establishment of the **North Atlantic Treaty Organization**).

Adenauer was also awarded the **Charlemagne Award** (or Karlspreis) in 1954 for his outstanding contributions to the process of European **integration**.

advocate general A part of the staff of the European **Court of Justice**. Currently there are eight advocates general – five are appointed from the largest member **states**, the remainder come from the other member states in rotation. Advocates general are lawyers of high standing within the legal profession. Each appointment is for a renewable six-year term. The role of an advocate general is to present an 'opinion' to the Court on each case to which they have been assigned. This 'opinion' must be presented impartially.

African, Caribbean and Pacific (ACP) countries The ACP countries, as the name suggests, comprise countries from Africa, the Caribbean and the Pacific. These countries are mostly former colonies of the European **states** and are under-developed economically. Thus former colonies such as Australia and New Zealand are excluded from the ACP group. There are about 80 ACP countries, which receive developmental aid from the **European Union**

(EU). This aid will total around €23 billion during the period 2008–13.

The EU and its predecessors have always had some sort of commitment to their former colonies via treaties such as **Yaoundé**, **Lomé** and **Cotonou**. However, it could be pointed out that the EU would never enter into a trade agreement unless it was of benefit to the EU.

Agenda 2000 Part of the reforms of the **Common Agricultural Policy** (CAP) that were agreed in 1999 and covered the period 2000–6. This reform needs to be seen in the context of the **enlargement** of the **European Union** (EU) in May 2004. It cut the amount of subsidy for farmers in a number of different areas, although there were generous compensation packages. The cuts in subsidies for farmers were part of a change in the payment scheme. Rather than price supports, which guaranteed minimum prices for farmers, there was a move towards direct payments. Such a move had already been started by Ray MacSharry (Commissioner for Agriculture in the early 1990s) but Agenda 2000 accelerated the process. There was also an increase in planned spending for the **Structural Fund**s and the **Cohesion Fund**. Agenda 2000 also introduced the **PHARE Programme** to help the applicant **state**s from Eastern Europe prepare for joining the EU.

Alliance of Liberals and Democrats for Europe The third largest grouping in the **European Parliament**, after the **European People's Party and European Democrats** and the **Socialist Group in the European Parliament**. The group was formerly known as the European Liberal Democrat and Reform Group. It is a pro-European grouping which is, for the most part, right of centre in its political outlook, although the current leader of the group, Graham Watson, is a member of the British Liberal Democratic Party (which is a left-of-centre political party). Yet the group is far more complicated in its ideological underpinnings. Economically, it supports policies such as privatisation and would therefore be perceived as being a right-wing grouping. However, their social policies are far more centre-left – for example, promoting multiculturalism with a conference entitled Unity in Diversity in January 2005. A majority of the group's **Members of the European Parliament** are also supportive of Turkish membership of the **European Union**.

Amsterdam Treaty   see **Treaty of Amsterdam**

assent procedure   Part of the legislative process. It is a particular power given to the **European Parliament** over particular policy areas, for example **enlargement**. The power was granted under the **Single European Act** in 1987. Ultimately, the assent procedure gives the European Parliament a 'Yes/No' option, which places it on a par with the other institutions. Thus the European Parliament, by refusing to give assent, could block any further enlargements of the **European Union**. There is no option to amend any proposals.

awkward partner   This label has been used to describe British membership of the **European Union** (EU). Another is **reluctant European**. The label 'awkward partner' acknowledges that Britain is part of the EU but that Britain – or more specifically British governments – seem less than enthused about the European project. Part of this can be attributed to the British model of politics, which is confrontational. Parliament, for example, is divided into Her Majesty's Loyal Government and Her Majesty's Loyal Opposition. Government proposes legislation,

Opposition opposes it. Continental Europe, on the other hand, tends to adopt a far more consensual approach to politics – the idea of trying to get all parties to agree. This is a feature of coalition governments. The EU utilises this idea of developing consensus, which is something that does not sit comfortably in the British model of politics. The 'awkward partner', therefore, seems to simply oppose many ideas put forward by the EU rather than trying to work towards a compromise. Margaret **Thatcher** was probably the most awkward of all British prime ministers, with tales of her 'handbagging' her European partners at summit meetings.

B

Barroso, José Manuel (1956–)   Barroso is the current President of the European **Commission**. Prior to this, he was prime minister of Portugal (2002–4). He took over as President in 2004. Barroso's tenure as President has seen a number of problems. The first was in getting the **European Parliament** to accept his proposed Commission. They refused over one particular appointment. This was Rocco Buttiglione who was the Italian Commissioner and it had been proposed that he become the Commissioner for Justice, Freedom and Security. Buttiglione was, however, opposed to gay rights and women's rights – something about which many **Members of the European Parliament** felt quite strongly. Rather than give Buttiglione a different portfolio, Barroso decided to back the proposed candidate with the specific portfolio. The rules of appointment are such that the European Parliament had to reject the entire Commission rather than the specific candidate – and they did so. Buttiglione stood down but this rejection suggested a degree of impotence on the part of Barroso.

Other problems for Barroso have included the proposed **European constitution,** and in particular its rejection in some member **states,** reform of the **Common Agricultural Policy,** and reform of the **budget.**

It was also hoped that Barroso would be a somewhat stronger leader of the Comission than his two predecessors – Jacques **Santer** and Romano **Prodi.** Under Santer and Prodi, it was felt that the **European Union** (EU) merely drifted along. There appeared to be no strong agenda towards greater **integration,** despite the introduction of the **Euro** and the work towards further **enlargement** of the EU.

Benelux Customs Union   Created between Belgium, the Netherlands and Luxembourg, this **customs union** came into effect in 1948 and became the Benelux Economic Union ten years later. It has been seen as a prototype for the development of the **European Union.** What is clear is that it signalled the integrationist tendencies of these three **states.**

British rebate   This is one of the most contentious parts of the **budget** of the **European Union** (EU). It was negotiated at the **Fontainebleau Summit** in 1984. Margaret **Thatcher** won a refund of two-thirds of Britain's budgetary contribution. The reasons for such a refund included Britain's small, but very efficient, farming sector which received very little from the **Common Agricultural Policy** (CAP), especially when compared to the amount of money that the French received. Britain also imported large amounts of agricultural produce from the Commonwealth. This should have been resolved in the seven-year transition period after British accession to the then **European Economic Community.** Initially, Britain was to receive **European Regional Development Fund** monies to help the weaker parts of the British economy. However, as this scale of funding was not as large as expected, an alternative solution had to be found. Ultimately, this was the British rebate.

What is of concern is that over twenty years later, Britain is still receiving the rebate. The British economy is one of the strongest in the EU but this has not stopped successive British governments from drawing a **red line** over any negotiations about the rebate. The Labour Government under Tony Blair actually surrendered part of the rebate in the budgetary negotiations in 2005. This was in return for a pledge to reform the CAP at the next round of budgetary negotiations in five years' time.

budget   The budget of the **European Union** (EU) is very complex. It is important to examine the sources of revenue and the way in which the budget is spent, as well as the way in which the budget is approved by the different EU institutions.

Each member **state** contributes an amount which is roughly in proportion to their population size within the EU. There is a limit on the size of the budget, currently at 1.27 per cent of the total GNP (Gross National Product) of the EU. This means that the budget for the EU is currently around €100 billion. To put this into context, the United Kingdom budget is more than six times larger than that of the EU.

It is the way in which the EU budget is spent that causes the most controversy. Almost half of it is currently spent on the **Common Agricultural Policy** and agriculture-related areas. This is despite the fact that the agricultural sector comprises around 5 per cent of the EU workforce. The **Structural Fund**s and the **Cohesion Fund** take up around a quarter of the budget between them. The remainder is spent on other policies, administration of the EU, money for applicant countries via the **PHARE** project and so on.

There is a great deal of debate as to how the budget is allocated. Some member states are net contributors to the budget, others are net beneficiaries. The countries that give more (such as the UK) wish for the allocation of funds to be re-evaluated. Other member states (such as France) are less enthused about such an idea. Newer member states, particularly those in Eastern Europe, would like to see the budget increased in size. Considering that all of the East European countries who joined in 2004 are, however, net beneficiaries of the budget, and that the net contributors would be increasing their contribution, this proposal is not likely to go very far.

One aspect that is under pressure is the **British rebate**. Most member states would like to see this particular anomaly ended. However, for all British governments, this has been a **red line** issue and not up for negotiation.

C

CAP   see **Common Agricultural Policy**

CFSP   see **Common Foreign and Security Policy**

Charlemagne Award   Also known as the Karlspreis, this award is presented each year in Aachen, Germany, to someone who has made a substantial contribution to the process of European **integration**. The recipient of the award does not have to be a European, as can be seen with Bill Clinton receiving the award in 2000. Many prominent Europeans have received the award, including Jean **Monnet**, Paul-Henri **Spaak** and Jacques **Delors**.

Charter of Fundamental Rights   Part of the draft **constitution** of the **European Union** (EU). The Charter was originally approved at the **Treaty of Nice** in 2000, although it was non-binding on members. Had the constitution been ratified in all member **state**s, the Charter would probably have had the status of a Bill of Rights. Of all the EU institutions, the **Court of Justice** is the most eager to see the Charter ratified. The belief is that it will explicitly detail our fundamental rights. However, there is a concern that the Charter might be a little too dogmatic in detailing the rights of people, and that, like the Bill of Rights in the USA, it might be very difficult to amend. The seven chapters of the Charter of Fundamental Rights are:

1. Dignity
2. Freedoms
3. Equality
4. Solidarity
5. Citizens' rights
6. Justice
7. General provisions

closer co-operation   see **enhanced co-operation**

co-decision   The power of co-decision was introduced through the **Treaty on European Union**. It means that the **European Parliament** and the **Council of Ministers** have become almost equal partners in the legislative process of the **European Union**. In effect, the European Parliament is consulted on three occasions (similar to the three readings of a bill in the British House of Commons) on legislative proposals. The steps are consultation, co-operation and co-decision. If the **opinion**s of the European Parliament are not accepted, the Council of Ministers is now compelled to explain its reasoning. The Council of Ministers must also be unanimous in its rejection of the advice of the European Parliament.

Cohesion Fund   Established in 1992. It runs in tandem with the other **Structural Fund**s. The objective of the Fund is to compensate poorer countries in the **European Union** which may be suffering as a result of increased competition. There is a threshold for eligibility. A country needs to have a GDP of less than 90 per cent of the EU average. Until 2006, four countries gained Cohesion Fund monies: Greece, Ireland, Spain and Portugal. Ireland no longer qualifies for the funding, but the other three countries (along with the twelve new member **state**s) still receive money. Between 2000 and 2006, the four eligible countries received €18 billion. The money had to be spent on projects related to the environment and improving transportation infrastructure.

Cohesion Policy   This policy is about reducing disparities across the **European Union** (EU). These disparities can be social or economic. Thus the focus can be on infrastructure, job creation and job training or investment in social projects. Funding for this policy comes from a number of sources, including the **Structural Fund**s and the **Cohesion Fund**. It totals around a quarter of the EU **budget** spending. The problem with this policy is that with the last two **enlargement**s of the EU, the disparities between the richest and poorest countries have increased drastically. As a result, the majority of Cohesion Policy monies will be spent in these countries. This could be to the detriment of some of the poorer regions in the wealthier member **state**s.

comitology   This is **European Union** (EU) jargon for the complex committee procedures which are utilised to work out the rules and **regulations** to implement EU legislation. In effect, they inspect the policy proposals of the **Commission**. Much of this can be seen as the consequence of a power struggle between the Commission, the **Council of Ministers** and the **European Parliament** over policy implementation. Originally, the Council of Ministers was seen as the most important body in policy implementation but this has now been shared with the Commission due to the volume of legislation. The European Parliament obtained a role here as well through the **Treaty on European Union** and the introduction of the **co-decision** procedure. This involvement has made the comitology system even more complex.

The committees are normally chaired by representatives of the Commission. The membership, however, is made up of national representatives. This often causes friction over any supranational moves by the Commission.

Under the jargon of comitology, there are three types of committee: advisory committees; management committees; and regulatory committees.

Advisory committees make **recommendations** to the Commission. This can be seen as providing some advice on particular policies. They are the least powerful of the committees, as recommendations are non-binding.

Management committees, which were first established in 1962 with regard to the **Common Agricultural Policy**, are somewhat more powerful. If the specific committee objects to a policy (under **qualified majority voting** rules), then the policy proposal must go to the Council of Ministers for approval.

A similar system applies to regulatory committees, although here the European Parliament must also be informed. If there is opposition from the Council of Ministers to the Commission's proposals, then the proposals must be sent back to the Commission for re-evaluation.

There is no obligation on the Commission to amend the proposals. Failure to do so, however, may result in a situation of gridlock, or an impasse between the Commission and the Council of Ministers.

Commission   This body is sometimes perceived as the civil service of the **European Union** (EU), although it is far more important. The Commission draws up legislative proposals for consideration by other EU institutions – most notable the **Council of Ministers** and the **European Parliament**. The Commission is also the '**guardian of the treaties**'. This means that the Commission tries to make sure that all member **state**s uphold both the letter and the spirit of the agreements made in key treaties (such as the **Treaty of Rome**, **Treaty on European Union** and so on). Commissioners are appointed by national governments, although they are supposed to work to further the aims of the EU, not national aims. The European Parliament has to approve the Commission before the Commissioners enter their posts.

A future concern for the Commission is the possible increased membership after any future **enlargement**s. Questions have been raised as to the extent to which the Commission has become too unwieldy with 27 Commissioners. Possible membership for Turkey and Croatia (or, for that matter, any other state) may lead to a total overhaul of Commission appointments. This may include breaking the link of each member having representation on the Commission.

Committee of Permanent Representatives (COREPER)   The body which assists the **Council of Ministers**. It comprises civil servants and diplomats who are there to assist their governments. They are the resident national representatives – for example, UKREP are the British Representatives.

Table C1   The Barroso Commission (January 2007)

Name	Country	Portfolio
José Manuel Barroso	Portugal	President
Margot Wallström	Sweden	Institutional Relations and Communications Strategy (Vice-President)
Günter Verheugen	Germany	Entreprise and Industry (Vice-President)
Jacques Barrot	France	Transport (Vice-President)
Siim Kallas	Estonia	Administrative Affairs, Audit and Anti-fraud (Vice-President)
Franco Frattini	Italy	Justice, Freedom and Security (Vice-President)
Viviane Reding	Luxembourg	Information Society and Media
Stavros Dimas	Greece	Environment
Joaquín Almunia	Spain	Economic and Monetary Affairs
Danuta Hübner	Poland	Regional Policy
Joe Borg	Malta	Fisheries and Maritime Affairs
Dalia Grybauskaite	Lithuania	Financial Programming and Budget
Janez Potocnik	Slovenia	Science and Research
Ján Figel'	Slovakia	Education, Training and Culture
Markos Kyprianou	Cyprus	Health
Olli Rehn	Finland	Enlargement
Louis Michel	Belgium	Development and Humanitarian Aid
László Kovács	Hungary	Taxation and Customs Union
Neelie Kroes-Smit	Netherlands	Competition
Marian Fischer Boel	Denmark	Agriculture and Rural Development

Table C1   (*continued*)

Name	Country	Portfolio
Benita Ferrero-Waldner	Austria	External Relations and European Neighbourhood Policy
Charlie McCreevy	Ireland	Internal Market and Services
Vladimír Špidla	Czech Republic	Employment, Social Affairs and Equal Opportunities
Peter Mandelson	UK	Trade
Andris Piebalgs	Latvia	Energy
Leonard Orban	Romania	Multilingualism
Meglena Kuneva	Bulgaria	Consumer Protection

Much of COREPER's work is secret. The Permanent Representatives (who are the national ambassadors to the **European Union**) and their teams meet with their counterparts on a regular basis – normally weekly. In general terms, these Permanent Representatives do all of the legwork prior to a meeting of the Council of Ministers.

Since 1962, with the huge increases in work for COREPER, the body has been divided in two. COREPER 1 comprises the Deputy Permanent Representatives, while COREPER 2 comprises the Permanent Representatives. There is a rigid division of work. Areas designated to COREPER 1 include fisheries, education, consumer affairs and health. COREPER 2 covers areas such as the **budget**, justice and home affairs, the **Structural** and **Cohesion Funds,** and accession. There is no overlap of policy responsibilities.

Committee of Regions   This is an advisory body created by the **Treaty on European Union**. Delegates come from regional and local government from all member states. The larger member states (France, Germany, Italy and the United Kingdom) have twenty-four delegates each, while the smallest (Malta) has five. The Committee of Regions must be consulted in a number of specified policy areas (particularly in areas that affect regional or local government), although its advice is purely advisory and need not be heeded. However, the existence of this body highlights the importance of **regionalism** and **subsidiarity** to the **European Union**.

Common Agricultural Policy (CAP)   The CAP was part of the **Treaty of Rome**, although it did not formally come into existence until 1962. The aim was to protect European farming livelihoods, while also trying to make Europe self-sufficient in food production. The key points of the CAP as laid down in the Treaty of Rome are:

- to increase agricultural productivity by promoting technical progress and by ensuring the rational development of agricultural production;
- to ensure a fair standard of living for the agricultural community, in particular by increasing the individual earnings of persons working in agriculture;
- to stabilise markets;
- to assure the availability of supplies; and
- to ensure that the supplies reach the consumers at reasonable prices.

In order to make the CAP work it was necessary to establish a **single market** for agriculture across all of the then **European Economic Community** (EEC). Linked to this was free trade in agricultural goods and common prices across all member states. What the CAP also tried to do was to guarantee minimum prices for farmers.

Prices were set by the EEC. If they fell lower than the minimum then the EEC made up the shortfall in farmers' incomes. To help in this, the idea of **community preference** was introduced.

All of the expenditure on agriculture comes from the **European Agricultural Guidance and Guarantee Fund** (EAGGF). This has taken up a sizeable proportion of the **budget** of the **European Union** (EU). Currently, it takes up just under half of the budget. Originally, the more farmers produced, the more they were paid. This led to overproduction in a number of areas, for example beef, cereals, dairy and wine.

Reform of the CAP has been high on the agenda of many member states – most notably Britain. A key reform has been the idea of **decoupling**. This was introduced by Ray MacSharry in the early 1990s. It started to break down the relationship between production and funding. Other reforms have included set-aside, whereby farmers took around 15 per cent of their land out of production. Farmers were compensated for set-aside – and it actually cost the EU more than had the land been left in production.

More recently, the **Agenda 2000** reforms have resulted in changes to the CAP. There are likely to be further reforms to the CAP, most probably to be introduced in 2014 when the ten states which joined in 2004 become eligible for full EU funding.

common commercial policy   This common policy focuses on the **common external tariff** and the **quota**s of goods that can enter the **European Union** (EU). Over time the remit of this policy has been broadened to include regulatory issues such as product conformity. The idea here is to make sure that products entering the EU market conform to such things as EU safety standards. However, as trading moves from goods to services, it is becoming more difficult to monitor and implement the policy.

common external tariff   A common external tariff is necessary to enable the **single market** to function effectively and efficiently. Any goods entering the **European Union** (EU) will have to pay the same **tariff**, regardless of which country they enter. The aim is to protect all member **states** from non-EU imports and to enable **community preference** to function more effectively.

Common Fisheries Policy   Although such a policy was raised in the **Treaty of Rome**, it was not until 1983 that the Common Fisheries Policy came into being. It focuses on preserving fishing stocks and the marine ecosystem, as well as the rights of consumers and those employed in the fishing industry. Unlike the **Common Agricultural Policy**, there is no guaranteed minimum income for those employed in fishing, nor is there a link between production and funding. There is a wholly different emphasis for the Common Fisheries Policy. This can be seen by examining the key policy areas, as detailed in Table C2.

The current focus of the Common Fisheries Policy is on **sustainable development** in fishing. Linked in with this is the protection of the environment. It is not just a question of keeping fishing stocks at a sustainable level, but also of ensuring that the different industries linked to fishing take care of the environment. The idea is to protect the aquaculture. Thus there are concepts such as 'polluter pays' and severe penalties for **over-fishing**, illegal fishing and discards (fish and molluscs which have been caught but thrown back). The inspection processes for the Common Fisheries Policy have also been improved.

Table C2   Policy areas of the Common Fisheries Policy

Access and conservation

- EU 200-mile zone for all EU fishermen
- 12-mile limit on own shores for member states
- All conservation levels to be agreed at the EU level
- National quotas established to protect fish stocks – these are known as Total Allowable Catches (TACs)

Market management
This covers:

- Price system
- Marketing arrangements
- External trade policy

Structural measures
Funding is available from the EU budget for:

- Processing and marketing development projects
- Conversion and modernisation schemes
- Redeployment

External negotiations

- Negotiations with non-EU states on fishing, and in particular on access to EU waters

Common Foreign and Security Policy (CFSP)   The CFSP forms the **second pillar** of the **European Union** (EU). In general terms, it covers how the EU conducts foreign affairs. The idea of the CFSP is to encourage co-operation between member **state**s on foreign-policy matters. Unlike other common policies, this one is co-ordinated by the **Council of Ministers**, not the **Commission**. It has its origins in **European Political Co-operation**, although everything was formalised under CFSP in the **Single European Act**.

While many other common policies, such as the **Common Agricultural Policy (CAP)**, are seen as steps towards **supranationalism**, the CFSP is far more **intergovernmental**. This means that national interest tends to be put above a common EU interest. Changes were made in the **Treaty of Amsterdam** (1999) which curtailed some aspects of national interest with the reduction of unanimous voting. No longer was it possible for a single member state to **veto** any CFSP proposals. Instead, the option of abstention was included, rather than simple support or opposition to any proposals.

The CFSP is still evolving. It has moved beyond simple security and foreign-policy issues to a broader remit, including humanitarian aid. The creation of a **European Rapid Reaction Force** under the **European Security and Defence Policy** has demonstrated the willingness of the EU to act collectively on foreign-policy issues. However, issues such as Iraq or the Israeli invasion of Lebanon have highlighted the inability of the EU to present a **common position** on such divisive issues.

common market   A term used to describe the original **European Economic Community** (EEC). There was always the suggestion of a **single market** for all participating members of the EEC in name if not in deed. The idea was that there would be a gradual **harmonisation** of customs duties and the establishment of a **common external tariff**. Internally, all trade barriers were to be removed. Arguably this has been achieved through the development of the single market, along with the introduction of the **Euro**.

common position   This is a step short of a common policy. A common position can be established by the **European Union** (EU) but it is very difficult to enforce. A common position tends to encourage, but cannot compel, all EU states to work together. The development of a common position can best be seen through the **Common Foreign and Security Policy** where national interest sometimes overrides community interest.

common strategy   This is an instrument of the **Common Foreign and Security Policy**, which was developed in the **Treaty of Amsterdam**. The **Council of Ministers** co-ordinates the CFSP and attempts to develop a **common position** on a particular issue or concern. From this the common strategy will then evolve. This could include things such as timescale, aims and objectives, and how the **European Union** and the member **states** may deal with the issue or concern.

Community Charter of the Fundamental Social Rights of Workers   see **Social Chapter**

community preference   If there is a choice between an agricultural product from the **European Union** (EU) and that of a non-EU **state**, community preference means that you should buy the Community product. To ensure this happens there is a common **tariff** barrier around the EU to make sure that the non-EU competition is of a higher price.

competence   The term used to describe the allocation of powers – specifically, the areas where member **states** have handed over policy-making powers to the **European Union** (EU). In these particular areas, EU law overrides national law, should the two conflict. The EU is considered to have 'competence' in these areas. However, according to the draft **constitution**, any areas not specifically mentioned as being EU 'competences' should remain under national control.

Competition Policy   The origins of the Competition Policy can be seen in the **Treaty of Paris**. It is also mentioned in the **Treaty of Rome**, where there is a focus upon the **common external tariff** and trade with non-member states. The Competition Policy aims to prevent distortions in competition between private businesses or within the public sector. Thus there are two parts to the Competition Policy. The first focuses upon the private sector; the second focuses upon the activities of the **state** and bodies sponsored by the state.

Competition Policy covers a wide range of issues. The main areas are:

- *Anti-trust and cartels*
  Here, focus is upon preventing businesses from working together to fix prices. It also prevents businesses with a dominant market position from eliminating any competition.
- *Merger control*
  In this area the Competition Policy ensures that any proposed mergers are not harmful for competition. If a proposed merger will stifle competition then the **Commission** may ban or impose conditions upon such a merger.
- *Liberalisation*
  This focuses upon opening up markets to new businesses to encourage greater competition.
- *State aids*
  The Commission monitors all of the different forms of aid that a state may give to businesses. This could include subsidies, tax breaks and so on. If the aid is not in the interests of the **European Union** (EU), then the state may be prevented from giving aid.

Competition Policy is also applicable beyond the EU. The principles behind the Competition Policy are built into many trade agreements with non-EU states. This is to prevent multi-national businesses taking advantage of anti-competitive practices in developing countries.

confederalism   Arguably, this term is used to describe a loose form of **federalism**. Under a confederal system (or confederation), the centre has far fewer powers than the regions. In the case of the **European Union** (EU), it would mean that the individual member **states** would have far greater powers than the EU institutions.

constitution   A constitution can be described as the 'rules of the political game'. Just as the rules of association football govern all aspects of the game, so a constitution covers all aspects of how politics operates in a country. A constitution allocates power to different institutions; it covers how people interact with these institutions and how the institutions can be held to account. A constitution can be written (as in the United States of America), unwritten, or partially written (as in the United Kingdom). It can be codified (written down in a single document, as is the case in the USA) or uncodified (not written down in a single document, as is the case in the UK).

The **European Union** (EU) does not have a formal codified constitution. An attempt was made by Valéry **Giscard d'Estaing** to do so. It was agreed in Brussels in June 2004 but then had to be put to all member **states** for ratification. There were some contentious ideas in the draft **European constitution**, such as an EU foreign minister and a president of the **European Council**. However, much of the constitution was little more than tidying up legislation that already existed. In effect, the draft constitution clarified the relationship between the EU institutions and the member states. It also included an action plan for the EU should a member state withdraw. In this respect, it was akin to a formal constitution. It allocated power between the member states and the EU; it clarified how the people of Europe could interact with the EU as well as how the EU would be held to account.

The draft constitution has been ratified in some member states but was defeated in national **referendum**s in both France and the Netherlands. Some member states, such as Britain and Poland, have yet to attempt ratification. At the time of writing the feeling is that the constitution is 'dead in the water'. However, there have been suggestions that the President of the **Commission**, José Manuel **Barroso**, was examining ways to resurrect the proposals, but in a more user-friendly format.

constitutional treaty   see **constitution** and **European constitution**

constructive abstention   This was introduced in the **Treaty of Amsterdam**, along with the **emergency brake** to replace unanimous voting on the **Common Foreign and Security Policy** (CFSP). Constructive abstention meant that a member **state** had the opportunity to 'not support' a policy proposal. Under unanimous voting, the options were to either 'support' or 'oppose' the proposal. Constructive abstention enables up to one third of member **state**s to abstain without defeating the policy proposal.

consultation procedure   This process enables the **European Parliament** to give an **opinion** on a policy proposal from the **Commission**. The **Council of Ministers** must consult with the European Parliament but is under no obligation to follow the Parliament's position. Today, this is the first step in the legislative process. Subsequently there is **co-operation** and **co-decision**.

convergence criteria   These were a range of prerequisites that all participating member **states** were required to meet as part of the move to adopting the **Euro**. They included placing a limit on the national budget deficit of each member state (to be set at less than 3 per cent of the state's gross domestic product, GDP); a limit on the level of public debt (at less than 60 per cent of GDP); limiting rates of inflation (to 1.5 per cent of the average of the three participating member states with the lowest rates); and placing limits on long-term rates of interest (to within 2 per cent of the average of the three participating member states with the lowest rates). Added to all of this, each participating member state had to keep their exchange rates within the approved **Exchange Rate Mechanism** (ERM) fluctuation margins for two years. In theory, failure to comply with the convergence criteria meant that a member state would not be allowed to join the Euro. However, failure to comply with the first two of the above criteria did not necessarily mean exclusion. If a state could demonstrate that it was a temporary error, then a waiver could be granted.

co-operation procedure   This was introduced by the **Single European Act**. It increased the influence of the **European Parliament** in the legislative process, by giving it, in effect, a second reading. If the **opinions** of the European Parliament, as expressed in the **consultation procedure**, are not accepted, the co-operation procedure enables the Parliament to express their opinion about the position of the **Council of Ministers**. To amend or reject proposals from the Council of Ministers, the European Parliament requires the support of an absolute majority of its members. However, the Council of Ministers may still **veto** the proposals of the Parliament. After this process, there is now a third reading – the **co-decision** process.

Copenhagen criteria   The criteria that any member **state** must meet to be able to join the **European Union**. There are political criteria (democracy, civil rights, respect for minorities) and economic criteria (the economy must be market dominated), as well as an applicant state having the ability to cope with the rigours of membership and adopting the *acquis communautaire*. The criteria were decided in 1993 at a **European Union** (EU) summit in Copenhagen. At that time, no emphasis was given to any aspect of the criteria. Since then, the **Commission** has placed greater emphasis upon the political criteria.

One interesting aspect of these criteria, which is often underplayed, is that the EU has to demonstrate that it can include the new members while continuing with the programme of **integration**. Thus the Copenhagen criteria place requirements on the applicant state(s) as well as the EU.

COREPER   see **Committee of Permanent Representatives**

Cotonou Agreement   The Cotonou Agreement follows on from the **Yaoundé Convention** and the **Lomé Convention**. Currently, 77 **African, Caribbean and Pacific countries** are covered by this agreement. The agreement covers politics, trade and development, with an overarching aim of eliminating poverty in signatory countries. The political aspects include promoting democratic participation, protecting human rights and so on. Failure to comply could result in economic sanctions being implemented and suspension from the agreement. From the trade perspective, the Cotonou Agreement encourages all signatories to promote free trade and integrate themselves into the global economy. This is done by eliminating trade barriers, promoting competition and so on. The development aspect may be perceived as being a result of the other two aspects. With improved political structures and a growing economy, there should be a knock-on effect of social improvement, such as improving standards of living and infrastructure. This should result in the eventual elimination of poverty.

A significant difference between the Cotonou Agreement and its predecessors is its time span. Whereas both Yaoundé and Lomé were five-year agreements which were then renewed, Cotonou is expected to last for twenty years (although it will be reviewed every five years).

Council of Economic and Finance Ministers   see **Ecofin**

Council of Ministers   The Council of Ministers (also known as the Council of the European Union) is considered to be the most important body within the **European Union** (EU). In effect it is the law-making body of the EU, although it is now a **co-decision**-maker with the **European Parliament**. When the Council of Ministers meets, each member **state** sends a representative. Thus when agriculture is under discussion, each member state will send their Minister of Agriculture; when the issue is transport, the Transport Ministers will attend, and so on. It could be argued that there are in fact multiple Councils of Ministers.

Decisions can be taken by **simple majority voting, qualified majority voting** or **unanimity**. Each country receives a number of votes, weighted against their population size (see Table C3). What is interesting about the weightings is that they still count against the larger member states. Per head of population, Malta and Luxembourg have far more votes than Germany.

To further complicate matters, the Council of Ministers utilises a rotating presidency. Each member state holds the

Table C3   Weights of votes in the Council of Ministers (2007)

Country	Population (millions)	Votes
Germany	82	29
UK	60	29
France	59	29
Italy	58	29
Spain	39	27
Poland	39	27
Romania	22	14
Netherlands	16	13
Greece	11	12
Belgium	10	12
Portugal	10	12
Czech Republic	10	12
Hungary	10	12
Sweden	9	10
Austria	8	10
Bulgaria	8	10
Denmark	5	7
Finland	5	7
Slovakia	5	7
Ireland	4	7
Lithuania	4	7
Latvia	2	4
Slovenia	2	4
Estonia	1	4
Cyprus	0.7	4
Luxembourg	0.4	4
Malta	0.4	3
Total	*492*	*345*

presidency for six months at a time. With the current 27 member states, this means a country holds the presidency for 6 months in every 13.5 years. Dates of the presidency are shown in Table C4.

Table C4   Rotation of the presidency of the Council of
Ministers

Country	Date of presidency
Germany	January–June 2007
Portugal	July–December 2007
Slovenia	January–June 2008
France	July–December 2008
Czech Republic	January–June 2009
Sweden	July–December 2009
Spain	January–June 2010
Belgium	July–December 2010
Hungary	January–June 2011
Poland	July–December 2011
Denmark	January–June 2012
Cyprus	July–December 2012
Ireland	January–June 2013
Lithuania	July–December 2013
Greece	January–June 2014
Italy	July–December 2014
Latvia	January–June 2015
Luxembourg	July–December 2015
Netherlands	January–June 2016
Slovakia	July–December 2016
Malta	January–June 2017
UK	July–December 2017
Estonia	January–June 2018
Bulgaria	July–December 2018
Austria	January–June 2019
Romania	July–December 2019
Finland	January–June 2020

When a country holds the presidency, this gives them the
opportunity to set the EU agenda. Thus when Britain held
the presidency in 2005, the focus was on future Turkish
membership of the EU, as well as reform of both the
budget and the **Common Agricultural Policy**.

The rotation of the presidency is very important. When a member holds the presidency in the second half of the year, their main objective will be to prepare the budget. In the first half of the year, agricultural spending is the important concern. Thus Britain held the presidency in the second half of 2005 and tried to prepare the budget. On the rotation as shown in Table C4, Britain will again hold the presidency in the second half of the year (in 2017). Assuming there are no changes to the system of a rotating presidency, the subsequent British presidency will be in the first half of the year.

The Council of Ministers is assisted by a body known as COREPER (**Committee of Permanent Representatives**). Each member state has its own COREPER. The UK, for example, has UK-REP.

The Council of Ministers is normally seen as part of the **intergovernmental** aspect of the EU. It is in this body that national concerns are raised and protected – sometimes at the expense of the EU. With the EU now having a membership of 27, it is becoming ever more difficult to protect national interests. Margaret **Thatcher** once complained that Britain had surrendered too much **sovereignty**. It is even more the case now than when Thatcher was speaking in the late 1980s that the only way to protect a country's sovereignty is to 'surrender' some of it. Except in cases of extreme national importance, where the **veto** can be used, a country can only achieve its objectives by working with other members.

Council of the European Union   see **Council of Ministers**

Court of Auditors   This body's sole responsibility is in examining the financial affairs of the **European Union** (EU). Unlike the **Court of Justice** or the **Court of First Instance**, the Court of Auditors is not a judicial court. It started operating in 1977, after the **European Parliament** was allocated power over the **budget**. The status of the Court of Auditors was improved in the **Treaty on European Union** – to the extent that it is on a par with the other EU institutions.

The membership of the Court of Auditors is currently 27 members, one from each member **state**. Members are appointed for a renewable six-year term, although they are all supposed to operate independent of their national governments. Eligibility for membership is dependent upon having experience of control over public funds. The **Council of Ministers** and the European Parliament have to approve all appointments.

The Court of Auditors produces a report on the budget every year. It examines how money has been spent and the extent to which goals have been achieved. In practice, this effectively means fighting potential fraud in the EU.

Court of First Instance   This body was created to assist the **Court of Justice** in 1988. The Court of First Instance deals with matters of fact, as opposed to legal interpretation. It now works independently of the Court of Justice. Its membership is currently made up of 27 judges, one from each member **state**.

Court of Justice   The Court of Justice – or the Court of Justice of the European Communities, to use its full title – is based in Luxembourg. Its role is as a final court of appeal. It also makes sure that all member **state**s uphold the treaties that have formed the **European Union**. It is not proactive, which means that it must be asked to investigate a particular issue. There are, however, restrictions on what the Court of Justice may investigate. It may only investigate matters that come under the **competence** of the EU. If it is a national, regional or local matter, then it is beyond the remit of the Court of Justice. This is the application of the concept **subsidiarity**. The Court of Justice deals with matters of law, as opposed to matters of fact.

The judges are assisted by eight **advocates general**, all of whom are appointed for renewable six-year terms. These appointments are based on judicial experience, rather than being political appointees. Their independence from their 'home' government is considered to be very important. This can be compared with the US Court of Justice where all appointments are 'political' rather than made on judicial merit.

Cresson, Édith (1934–) Former French prime minister Cresson (1991–2), as a member of the **Commission**, was charged with corruption. As a result, the entire Commission of Jacques **Santer** was forced to resign in 1999 – although the Commission resigned *en masse* before they were sacked. The corruption was not the first misdemeanour committed by Cresson.

Cresson wished to appoint a close friend (René Berthelot) as a personal adviser. However, due to his age, Berthelot was ineligible to be a member of a Commissioners cabinet. Cresson officially employed Berthelot as a visiting scientist, although his role was clearly that of a personal adviser. In 2004, the **Court of First Instance** investigated this case but decided not to take any further action as Berthelot was no longer employed by Cresson, and she was no longer a Commissioner.

The fraud case was somewhat more complicated. Vast sums of money had disappeared from a youth training programme over a number of years. Cresson had been made aware of the financial irregularities but had done nothing to remedy the situation. As a result, in 2006 the **Court of Justice** declared that Cresson had acted in breach of her duties as a Commissioner, but decided not to punish her any further.

customs union   The idea of a customs union is that there should be no trade barriers between member **states**. However, this could also apply to a **free trade area** such as the **European Free Trade Association**. Unlike a free trade area, a customs union also introduces a **common external tariff** and a **common commercial policy**. Thus any imports entering the customs union will have the same duty to be paid, regardless of which member state is the point of entry. Arguably, a customs union falls short of a **single market**. Whereas a customs union emphasises the free movement of goods, a single market introduces many other aspects such as the free movement of people, services and capital.

The **European Union** (EU) is no longer merely a customs union. It is now a single market, although all member states which have signed up to the **Euro** are, arguably, part of an economic union. Since the mid-1990s, the EU has established a customs union with Turkey. This agreement excludes agricultural products.

D

de Gaulle, Charles (1890–1970)   As President of France (1958–69), de Gaulle had a huge impact upon the development of the **European Economic Community** (EEC). He was supportive of the development of the organisation, but was extremely wary of any steps towards greater **integration**. The protection of French **sovereignty** was of paramount importance. This could be seen in his actions during the **empty chair crisis**. De Gaulle was also wary of British membership of the EEC. He saw Britain as looking across the Atlantic towards the USA rather than across the Channel to Europe. This fear of Britain as a Trojan Horse which would enable the USA to interfere in European matters was such that it effectively led to de Gaulle vetoing the first two applications for British membership of the EEC in 1963 and 1967. His fear and distrust of the USA also led to de Gaulle withdrawing France from the **North Atlantic Treaty Organization** (NATO).

De Gaulle saw a role for Europe as a balance between East and West during the cold war. A key part of this was the inclusion of Germany. De Gaulle and the West German Chancellor Konrad **Adenauer** established a **Franco-German axis** for the running of the EEC. This became a key aspect of the running of the EEC, and has remained so despite four rounds of **enlargement**.

decision   A type of act that can be passed by the **Council of Ministers**. Decisions are binding in every respect upon those to whom they are addressed (and nobody else). They can be directed against a member **state**, an organisation, or even an individual. Other acts include **directives**, **regulations**, **recommendations** and **opinions**.

decoupling   This was part of the plans developed by the European Commissioner for Agriculture, Ray MacSharry, in 1992 to reform the **Common Agricultural Policy**. It involved breaking the link between the amount of money paid to farmers and the amount that they produced. In effect, it was a move from price support to income support. This was taken further in the CAP reforms of 2003 which moved to a system of single farm payments, not in any way linked to production, that is, total decoupling.

deepening   This can be seen as a shorthand term for **integration**. The idea of deepening the **European Union** (EU) is all about drawing the member **state**s closer together – an **ever closer union**. This can be through member states ceding more powers to the EU, or enabling the EU to develop more in the way of common policies, **common position**s and **common strategy**. The opposite of deepening is **widening**.

Delors, Jacques (1925–)   Jacques Delors was President of the **Commission** from 1985 to 1995. While he was at the helm, the **Single European Act**, the **Treaty on European Union** and a timetable for adopting the **Euro** (the **Delors Plan**) were all established. All of these have been important in developing the **integration** of the **European Union** – and for this Delors received the **Charlemagne Award**. Delors was also a key player in persuading the European Union to introduce legislation promoting the social aspects of Europe. This is best exemplified by the **Social Charter** which was agreed at Maastricht along with the Treaty on European Union.

Many of Delors' ideas were seen as unpalatable by Margaret **Thatcher**. She saw Delors as trying to increase the role of the **state**, and possibly even developing a European superstate. Delors was eager to speed up the integration process, which included the completion of the **single market**. It was envisaged that the single market would also improve levels of competitiveness across all member states. To ensure this was a success, member states had to cede further powers to European institutions. Thatcher was supportive of the development of the single market but was far from enthused about ceding powers to Brussels.

Delors Plan   The timetable for moving from the **European Monetary System** (EMS) and the **Exchange Rate**

Mechanism (ERM) to a single currency for the **European Union**. It was detailed in the **Delors Report** (see Table D1).

Table D1   The Delors timetable for Economic and
                   Monetary Union

Stage 1.	**Closer co-operation** on macro-economic policy across all member states.
Stage 2.	Launch of the **European System of Central Banks (ESCB)**, co-ordinating monetary policy across all member states. Community institutions to be given greater supervisory powers. A narrowing of margins of fluctuation between currencies.
Stage 3.	Establishment of fixed exchange rates and introduction of a single currency. All monetary policy to be decided at the European level by the **European Central Bank**.

Originally, no actual dates were included for the movement to **Economic and Monetary Union**. The plan was eventually timetabled in the **Treaty on European Union**. Stage 1 was to be completed by 31 December 1993, Stage 2 by 31 December 1998, with Stage 3 commencing on 1 January 1999.

Delors Report   Although the Delors Report (1989) is credited as being the stepping stone towards monetary union, it did not specify whether such a union would ensure the success of the **single market**. It produced similar results to the **Werner Report** (1969). The Delors Report identified four basic elements of economic union, shown in Table D2. Of these, three were already in place. Only the fourth was lacking.

Although the Delors Report outlined the timetable to **Economic and Monetary Union** (see Table D1), no dates were included at the time. These came much later, in the **Treaty on European Union**.

Table D2   The basic elements of economic union (Delors Report)

1. A **single market**. Within this, people, goods and services should be able to move around freely.
2. **Competition Policy**. This should ensure that markets operate effectively and efficiently.
3. Structural change and regional development. The less well-off regions within the EU needed a boost to catch up with the better-off regions.
4. Co-ordination of macro-economic policy across all member states.

democratic deficit   This is a difficult term to explain, although at a basic level it suggests a lack of democracy. This could be because there is little or no electoral accountability, or a lack of **transparency** in the decision-making process – which again suggests a lack of accountability to the people. Only one institution within the **European Union** is directly accountable to the people. This is the **European Parliament**, which is held to account every five years in **direct elections**. All of the other institutions are either appointed (such as the **Commission**) or indirectly elected (such as the **Council of Ministers**). In the case of the Council of Ministers, most of the national representatives have been elected to their national assembly or parliament.

The problem is that there is no obvious way in which the democratic deficit can be addressed. Some suggestions have been to increase the powers of the European Parliament and possibly the **Committee of Regions** – with the latter becoming a form of second chamber to the European Parliament. However, this would result in less national involvement in the EU. The **intergovernmental** aspects of the EU would be reduced. If this were to happen, there is a feeling that a European superstate would be established. This would result in a loss of **sovereignty**, with national assemblies and parliaments possibly becoming redundant.

Even attempts to introduce more transparency in EU decision-making have struggled to address the democratic deficit. Each move seems to result in more administrators becoming involved in the EU and the whole system becoming overly bureaucratic.

direct election   An election to the **European Parliament**. Direct elections commenced in 1979. Prior to this, **Members of the European Parliament** (MEPs) were appointed from their national assemblies. Although there are direct elections to the European Parliament, no uniform electoral system is utilised, nor is there a single polling day. Since 1999, the only requirement of the electoral system has been that there is some form of proportional representation. Mainland Britain (including Gibraltar, which became part of the South West constituency in 2004) uses d'Hondt closed regional party lists, while Northern Ireland and the Republic of Ireland both use the single transferable vote (STV). Some member states, such as the UK, vote on a Thursday. Others, such as France, vote on a Sunday. No votes are counted in any member state until all polling stations in all member states are closed. Once elected, the MEPs do not sit in national blocks, but in **political group**s. These are known as ideological trans-national groups, or like-minded thinkers. They include the **European United Left**, the **European Liberal Democrat and Reform Group**, and the **European People's Party and European Democrats**.

directive   A type of act that can be passed by the **Council of Ministers**. Directives are binding on all member **state**s of the **European Union**. There is flexibility in the way in which member states can implement a directive. However, the aims and objectives of the legislation must be achieved.

Director-General The head of a **Directorate-General** (see Table D3) and similar to the senior civil servant in a government department in that he/she reports to a Commissioner. Some Directors-General, however, report to more than one Commissioner.

Table D3   The Directorates-General of the Commission and their Directors-General (April 2007)

Directorates-General	Directors-General
Agriculture and Rural Development	Jean-Luc Demarty
Budget	Luis Romero Requena
Competition	Philip Lowe
Development	Stefano Manservisi
Economic and Financial Affairs	Klaus Regling
Education and Culture	Odile Quintin
Employment, Social Affairs and Equal Opportunities	Nikolaus van der Pas
Enlargement	Michael Leigh
Enterprise and Industry	Heinz Zourek
Environment	Mogens Peter Carl
EuropeAid – Co-operation Office	Koos Richelle
External Relations	Eneko Landaburu
Fisheries and Maritime Affairs	Fokion Fotiadis
Health and Consumer Protection	Robert Madelin
Humanitarian Aid	António Cavaco
Informatics	Francisco García Morán
Information Society and Media	Fabio Colasanti
Internal Market and Services	Jörgen Holmquist
Interpretation	Marco Benedetti
Joint Research Centre	Roland Schenkel
Justice, Freedom and Security	Jonathan Faull
Personnel and Administration	Claude Chêne
Regional Policy	Dirk Ahner
Research	José Manuel Silva Rodríguez
Taxation and Customs Union	Robert Verrue
Trade	David O'Sullivan
Translation	Juhani Lönnroth
Transport and Energy	Mattias Ruete

Directorate-General   Each Directorate-General (DG) is responsible for a key policy area (see Table D3), some of which are tied to a specific member of the **Commission**. They function in a similar manner to ministerial departments in a national government. Each DG has its own **Director-General**, who works alongside one or more Commissioners. A Commissioner may have more than one DG within their portfolio, while a Director-General may report to more than one Commissioner.

What is of note is that the DG labels do not directly correspond to the different portfolios of the Commission. While there is some overlap, it can be difficult, at first sight, to work out which DG reports to which Commissioner (compare Table C1 with Table D3).

double majority voting   This system of voting has been utilised by the **Council of Ministers** since November 2004 (although it was agreed at the **Treaty of Nice** in 2001). In effect, it takes **qualified majority voting** (QMV) one step further. Under QMV, it is possible for a majority of votes to be achieved without a majority of countries or a majority of the **European Union** population actually supporting the legislative proposals. Double majority voting aims to prevent such a situation from occurring. A member **state** can request verification that a vote that is passed under QMV also represents at least 62 per cent of the EU population. If it does not then the legislative proposals may not be ratified. The draft **European constitution** had proposed to amend both QMV weightings which built in the double majority requirements.

See also: **unanimous decision-making**

dual mandate   Where a **Member of the European Parliament** (MEP) is also elected to their national parliament.

Officially, this is discouraged by the **European Parliament** and some countries, for example Italy, have made it illegal. However, there are still some MEPs who hold a dual mandate. Baroness Nicholson is an MEP for the Liberal Democrats, as is Baroness Ludford. Both also sit in the House of Lords. One former MEP, Ian Paisley, once held a triple mandate. He was an MEP, an MP and a member of the Northern Ireland Legislative Assembly, all at the same time.

E

EAGGF   see **European Agricultural Guidance and Guarantee Fund**

EC   see **European Community**

ECB   see **European Central Bank**

ECSC   see **European Coal and Steel Community**

Ecofin   An acronym for the Council of Economic and Finance Ministers. This is one of the different **Councils of Ministers** that exist. It is where all the national Finance Ministers meet. Arguably, it is one of the most important of all the Councils.

Economic and Monetary Union (EMU)   There have been several attempts to achieve monetary union in the **European Union** and its predecessors. There was the **Werner Plan**, the **European Monetary System**, and finally Economic and Monetary Union. EMU is perceived as being primarily about the development of the single currency – the **Euro**. It goes hand in hand with the completion of the **single market**. The **Treaty on European Union** set out the process of working towards EMU, building upon what already existed – the European Monetary System and the **Exchange Rate Mechanism**. The proposals in the Treaty on European Union were the formalisation of the **Delors Plan** (see Tables D1 and D2). Arguably, it is possible to have EMU without adopting a single currency. Fixed exchange rates could have worked just as easily, and without the cost of adopting the Euro.

Although the steps towards EMU appeared at first to be quite straightforward, this was not to be the case. Attempting to get the economies of 12 countries to **integrate** more fully turned out to be very difficult. There were specific **convergence criteria** on exchange rates to be met, as well as the creation of the **European System of Central Banks** and the **European Central Bank**. Added to this was the **Stability and Growth Pact,** where member **state**s were to attempt to control their budget deficits, as well as working towards achieving balanced budgets.

Yet EMU is not just about moving towards a single currency. Other related aspects also need to be included. If there is a single currency, then there needs to be a single authority (the European Central Bank) which sets monetary policy (governing the amount of money in circulation), and co-ordinated economic policies across all member states – especially at the macro-economic level. Macro-economic policies focus on the aggregate performance of the Euro-zone economy, including inflation, exchange rates, capital, employment and labour.

Economic and Social Committee   This body dates back to the **Treaty of Rome**, although its role has changed significantly over the years – in particular in the **Treaty on European**

Union and the **Treaty of Nice**. Like the **Committee of Regions**, the Economic and Social Committee has a fixed number of delegates from each member **state**. They are all unelected, but are drawn from different aspects of economic and social life: employers, employees and pressure groups. Each sub-group is of a similar size. The employers group is drawn from both the public and private sectors. The employees group is mostly drawn from trades unions. The pressure group covers all other aspects of life not covered by the previous two groups. This includes, for example, environmental groups, consumer groups, cultural organisations and social groups such as the elderly.

The Economic and Social Committee is a consultative body and its **opinion**s are not binding. However, its claim is that it draws in experts from the different aspects of social and economic life – acknowledging that elected politicians and civil servants are not always experts. This makes it a valuable asset to the **Commission** when drawing up legislative proposals.

economic partnership agreement   These agreements are aimed at improving the development and management of free trade between the **European Union** and developing countries around the world. The world is divided up into different regions, for example central Africa, west Africa and the Caribbean, each with different strategies to help the regions **integrate** into the world economy, while helping to eradicate poverty at the same time. These economic partnership agreements were developed alongside the **Cotonou Agreement** and are expected to be fully operational by 2008.

EDC   see **European Defence Community**

EEA   see **European Economic Area**

EEC   see **European Economic Community**

EFTA   see **European Free Trade Association**

emergency brake   This was introduced in the **Treaty of Amsterdam** in effect to replace unanimous voting in the **Council of Ministers** with regard to the **Common Foreign and Security Policy**. A second alternative was **constructive abstention**. Under the emergency brake, decision-making is taken under **qualified majority voting**. However, if a member **state** wishes to **veto** a proposal, the proposal is referred to the **European Council**. Should this happen the European Council has to operate under **unanimity**. In effect, this gives all member states the opportunity to rethink their positions.

empty chair crisis   This crisis was instigated by the then French President Charles **de Gaulle** in the mid-1960s. In 1965, there was a dispute over how the **Common Agricultural Policy** (CAP) should be funded. There had been suggestions that the **Commission** and the European Assembly (the forerunner of the **European Parliament**) should have the power to decide on CAP funding rather than the **Council of Ministers**. De Gaulle refused to accept such a move. At that time, the French held the presidency of the Council of Ministers. The French Government recalled its officials, leaving an empty chair presidency. This left the **European Economic Community** paralysed. No business was able to be conducted without the President of the Council of Ministers present. The situation was eventually resolved by the **Luxembourg Compromise**. The dispute over CAP funding was not revisited.

EMS   see **European Monetary System**

EMU   see **Economic and Monetary Union**

enhanced co-operation   This was originally known as closer co-operation. It was a process established in the **Treaty of Amsterdam** whereby member **states** wishing to further develop the **integration** process were able to do so. This would be integration beyond anything established in the various treaties. The idea was to present the **European Union** as being a flexible organisation, as opposed to a rigid one, where member states were able to introduce their own ideas on integration rather than being bound by the institutions of the EU. The process was relabelled enhanced co-operation in the **Treaty of Nice**. However, some important changes were introduced in the Treaty of Nice. The most notable of these was the removal of the right of any member state to **veto** any proposals under enhanced co-operation. This was similar to what had been introduced in the Treaty of Amsterdam – the **emergency brake** system – over the **Common Foreign and Security Policy** (CFSP).

enlargement   When the **European Union** (EU) increases the number of members. There have been several enlargements – 1973, 1981, 1986, 1995, 2004 and 2007. Table E1 lists these enlargements.

Prior to the first enlargement in 1973, there had been several attempts to increase the membership of the then **European Economic Community**. When the negotiations for the first enlargement took place, they were rather fraught as nobody appeared to know what was involved. This has changed significantly. There are the **Copenhagen criteria**, which have to be met by any applicant **state**. Added to this, all applicants must adopt the *acquis communautaire*. The size of the *acquis communautaire* has increased dramatically since the first enlargement,

Table E1   The enlargements of the European Union

Date	New members
1 January 1973	Denmark, Ireland, UK
1 January 1981	Greece
1 January 1986	Portugal, Spain
1 January 1995	Austria, Finland, Sweden
31 May 2004	Cyprus, Czech Republic, Estonia, Hungary, Latvia, Lithuania, Malta, Poland, Slovakia, Slovenia
1 January 2007	Bulgaria, Romania

highlighting the increased amount of legislation passed by the EU.

A number of other countries currently wish to join the EU. The most prominent of these are Croatia and Turkey. The enlargement to include these two states is tentatively proposed for 2014. Thereafter, further enlargements are perceived to be problematic. Strong cases could be presented for Bosnia or Serbia joining (subject to the Copenhagen criteria being met). However, other countries which have expressed an interest in membership include the Ukraine, Armenia and Morocco. This raises the issue of where the final boundaries of Europe lie.

Further reading: on the difficulties surrounding the negotiations for the 1973 enlargement, see U. Kitzinger, *Diplomacy and Persuasion: How Britain Joined the Common Market*, Thames and Hudson, 1973.

ENP   see **European Neighbourhood Policy**

EPC   see **European Political Co-operation**

EPP-ED   see **European People's Party and European Democrats**

ERDF   see **European Regional Development Fund**

ERM   see **Exchange Rate Mechanism**

ESCB   see **European System of Central Banks**

ESDP   see **European Security and Defence Policy**

EU   see **European Union**

Euratom   see **European Atomic Energy Community**

Euro   The term used for the single currency that has (to date) been adopted in 13 of the member **states** of the **European Union** (EU). There had been other plans to adopt a single currency, or at least a common currency unit. However, these fell by the wayside.

With regard to the Euro, the plans were evident in the **Delors Report**. During the 1990s, a range of moves transformed the **European Monetary System** and the **Exchange Rate Mechanism** into the **European Monetary Union,** which culminated in the creation of the Euro. There were some complications, as there were suggestions that some member states had fudged the **convergence criteria** in order to sign up to the Euro.

Since the Euro came into operation, it has endured a roller-coaster ride on the money markets. When it first came into being on 1 January 2002, the value of the Euro plummeted against the US dollar and UK sterling. Since then, it has regained that value and, in the case of the US dollar, is seen as being a stronger currency. Many non-EU states are now conducting their international trade in Euros rather than US dollars.

Europe of Democracies and Diversities   see **Independence/ Democracy Group**

European Agricultural Guidance and Guarantee Fund (EAGGF) This scheme was established in 1962. In effect, it pays out the money for the **Common Agricultural Policy**. The fund is administered by the **Commission** in conjunction with all member **states**. Each year the funds have to be cleared by the Commission. This involves assessing the completeness and accuracy of the accounts submitted by each member state.

The Guarantee aspect takes the larger share of the money. In 2004, it took up about 45 per cent of the total **European Union** (EU) **budget** – almost €45,000 million. Originally, the Guarantee aspect focused on the payments to farmers for their products. This has since been broadened to include aspects such as some veterinary expenditure and elements of rural development such as **Agenda 2000**. In 2005, this became a separate fund known as the EAGF (European Agricultural Guarantee Fund).

The Guidance aspect looks at issues to do with farming infrastructure. Surprisingly little of the EU's agricultural budget is spent here (around 8 per cent in 2004, which was €3,500 million). The focus here has been upon modernisation and diversification in farming, as well as reform of the agricultural sector. In 2005, the Guidance aspect was relabelled the EAFRD (European Agricultural Fund for Rural Development).

European Atomic Energy Community The European Atomic Energy Community (or Euratom) was set up alongside the **European Economic Community** in 1957. Its aim was to focus on developing a nuclear energy programme for economic purposes and possibly even to establish a **common market** in nuclear energy. There was a clear commitment that Euratom would focus on civilian and not military use of nuclear energy. The idea was for the six **founder member states** to pool their resources. In the 1950s, nuclear energy was hugely expensive for any one country. By pooling their resources, it was felt that all six **state**s would benefit from the investment.

The European Atomic Energy Community is still a separate entity. As a result of the **Merger Treaty** of 1967, it shares the same institutions as the **European Union** (EU). It is not actually part of the EU.

European Central Bank (ECB)   This body, which is based in Frankfurt, was created to formulate monetary policy for the **Euro**-zone countries. This means it focuses upon the amount of money in circulation in the Euro-zone and manipulates interest rates to control inflation. It came into being as part of stage 3 of **European Monetary Union**, as detailed in the **Delors Plan**. Along with the national central banks the ECB forms part of the **European System of Central Banks**.

The governing body of the ECB comprises the central bank governors from each participating **state**, along with a six-member full-time board. Each director serves a nonrenewable eight-year term. The current president of the ECB is Jean-Claude Trichet. In theory, this governing body is supposed to be wholly independent of all member states.

One major problem with the ECB is that it appears very difficult to hold it to account for any actions taken. The president of the ECB makes quarterly reports to the **European Parliament**, but the European Parliament has no means of input into the running of the ECB. To change the mandate of the ECB is very difficult. It would require **unanimity** from all member states and ratification in all national parliaments. In some cases, such as in Ireland, this would also mean holding a national **referendum** on the proposed changes. Thus the independence of the ECB is very clear but if anything goes wrong, it may be very difficult to rectify the mistakes.

European Coal and Steel Community (ECSC)   The original founding body of the **European Union** was the ECSC. It was created by the **Schuman** Plan, which led to the **Treaty of Paris**. The ECSC came into being in 1952 with a life expectancy of 50 years. All West European **states** were invited to participate, in particular the UK. However, in the end there were only six founder states. These were Belgium, France, Italy, Luxembourg, the Netherlands and West Germany.

The idea behind the creation of this **supranational** body was to make war unthinkable in Europe. By binding together major components of war (iron, steel and coal), for each member state, war would become impossible. There was also a degree of national self-interest among the participating states. Underpinning everything was the **Franco-German axis**. France and West Germany were the motor behind the ECSC. For West Germany, under the leadership of Konrad **Adenauer**, it was an opportunity for **integration** into Europe after the Second World War. For the other participating states, the emphasis was more upon trade and rebuilding Europe.

The ECSC also established its own supranational institutions. There was a High Authority, a **Council of Ministers**, an assembly and a **Court of Justice**. These institutions were the basis for the institutions that exist today. The High Authority became the **Commission**; the assembly evolved into the **European Parliament**.

With a 50-year lifespan built into the Treaty of Paris, the ECSC came to an end in 2002.

European Community (EC)   In 1975, the **European Economic Community** rebranded itself the European Community.

This was a clear acknowledgement that the organisation was far more than an economic 'club'. The EC was a political organisation as well as an economic one.

European constitution   More accurately, this should be labelled the *proposed* European **constitution** as it has not been ratified in all member states. The leaders of the **European Union** (EU) signed the Constitutional Treaty at a **European Council** meeting in October 2004, but it also needed to be ratified in every member state. Over half of the EU has ratified the constitution, although both France and the Netherlands returned negative **referendum** votes. Some states, such as the UK and Poland, have yet to attempt to ratify the proposed constitution and it appears most unlikely that they will even try in the near future.

The underpinning of the Constitutional Treaty was to streamline what already existed within the EU. All of the existing treaties, such as the **Treaty of Rome** and the **Treaty on European Union,** were to be brought under the Constitutional Treaty, along with introducing some institutional reform to the EU. Given the task of co-ordinating and writing the European constitution was Valéry **Giscard d'Estaing.**

One of the problems in drafting the EU constitution was that there was likely to be much opposition to whatever was proposed. For example, Giscard d'Estaing had to decide whether the constitution would be secular or religious. If it were to be the latter, would it be Christian or encompass all faiths? A Christian-based constitution would make it very difficult for Turkey to join the EU. In the end, the decision was taken to make the constitution secular.

Part of the proposed constitution included the **Charter of Fundamental Rights.** This would in effect give the

EU a formal bill of rights. Some member states, most notably the UK, were not overly enthusiastic about such a move. However, it was included as a key part of the draft constitution.

There were also proposed institutional changes within the constitution. The first of these was the removal of the rotating presidency of the **Council of Ministers**. This was to be replaced by a fixed presidency (the president elected by heads of state and government) for a renewable two-and-a-half-year term. Further, the voting rules within the Council of Ministers were to be simplified. There would also be an EU Foreign Minister. Other changes included the size of the **Commission**, which was to be reduced to two-thirds of its present size from 2014, while upper and lower limits on the number of **Members of the European Parliament** for the largest and smallest states would be introduced.

Currently, the European constitution is in a state of limbo. As it has not been ratified in all member states, it cannot become law. As both France and the Netherlands have voted against the proposed constitution, there is a feeling in some states that the constitution will not proceed any further. However, the President of the Commission, José Manuel **Barroso**, appears to have a scheme to resurrect the European constitution, but in a different guise.

The current German chancellor, Angela Merkl, is using her term as President of the European Council and of the Council of Ministers to try to resurrect aspects of the constitution. The key difference is that Merkl is only attempting to bring forward aspects of the constitution and thus not have to endure referendums in member states – most notably France and the Netherlands, but also Poland and the UK.

European Council   This body is sometimes considered to be the upper tier of the **Council of Ministers**, although it is not actually part of the Council of Ministers. It comprises the various heads of government and the president of the **Commission**, and has the power to overrule the Council of Ministers and the **European Parliament**. It normally meets twice a year, each time hosted by the country which has the presidency of the Council of Ministers. The European Council strives to develop a consensus among its members, rather than resorting to crude majoritarianism (via voting) or the use of national **veto**es. However, since the **Treaty of Amsterdam**, the European Council may utilise **qualified majority voting** on specific issues such as a member **state** deviating from the core values of the **European Union**.

The European Council was created in 1974, although it did not receive formal recognition until the **Single European Act** was passed. The idea behind the European Council was to provide a degree of leadership for the organisation as a whole. In effect it makes the key decisions on issues such as **integration**, foreign policy, issues to do with the **budget**, **enlargement** and so on. The European Council is often used to resolve disputes within the Council of Ministers. However, it could be argued that this actually undermines the authority of the Council of Ministers, as well as burdening the European Council with unnecessary problems that should have been resolved elsewhere.

European Defence Community (EDC)   A European defence pact drawn up in 1952 to include West Germany in the defence of Western Europe against possible Soviet invasion. It was never ratified. The architect of the plan was René **Pleven**, who was the French prime minister at the time. He proposed the plan in 1950.

Rather than having a remilitarised West Germany in the **North Atlantic Treaty Organization** (NATO), it was felt preferable to have a rearmed West Germany whose military was accountable to the EDC rather than to the West German government (but still within NATO control). All of the other participant countries in the EDC would have retained control over their own armed forces. The UK was keen on the EDC but wanted the **supranational** elements in the plan toned down before participating.

The EDC failed when the French government was unable to ratify the treaty. Many members of the French Assembly felt that the EDC might undermine French **sovereignty**. With the rejection of this treaty, the German government was able to retain control over its own military forces – something that the French had feared, which was why the EDC had been proposed!

European Development Fund   This fund is used to finance the **Cotonou Agreement**. It was established in 1958 and funded the precursors of Cotonou – **Yaoundé** and **Lomé**. However, there is a peculiarity with the fund in that it is not part of the **budget**, and will remain separate until 2008. From then, aspects of the European Development Fund will be included in the budget. It is not likely that all development fund monies will come from the budget until after 2013. Instead, it will continue to be funded by direct contributions from member **states**. Despite this point, the **European Parliament** has a degree of control over aspects of this fund under both the **assent procedure** and as a **co-decision-maker**. Between 2000 and 2007, the European Development Fund was worth around €13.5 billion. In addition, over the same time period, there was a further €10 billion which had not been spent over the previous time period (1995–2000).

European Economic Area (EEA)   The European Economic
Area (EEA) came into being in January 1994. It was
established to help prospective members prepare for
joining the **European Union** (EU). The original focus was
on **integration** of the **European Free Trade Association**
states into the single market, with the ultimate aim of
preparing them for membership. However, three of the
seven EFTA states joined the EU in 1995 and, arguably,
left the idea of the EEA redundant. Currently there are
four EFTA states – Iceland, Liechtenstein, Norway and
Switzerland. The Norwegians have voted against EU
membership twice (1972 and 1994). The Swiss have not
only refused to consider EU membership, but also held a
referendum which resulted in a vote against membership
of the EEA in 1992.

European Economic Community (EEC)   The **Treaty of
Rome** is the founding document of this organisation. The
origins of the treaty can be seen in the **Spaak** Report. The
EEC was set up in 1957 to integrate further the
economies of the **European Coal and Steel Community**
members beyond simply coal and steel – although it was
hoped that other countries (such as the UK) might also be
persuaded to participate. It was a very ambitious plan
which looked to create a common or **single market** (hence
the name **common market**) in which there would be free
movement of capital, goods, people and services. Ideas
such as the creation of a **Common Agricultural Policy**
and the development of social policies via a **social fund**
were also included. The overarching vision was that of
ever closer union. Originally there were six member
states. Through a series of **enlargement**s, membership
now stands at 27. However, the functioning of the EEC
has moved on significantly via, among others, the **Treaty
on European Union**, which established the union which

exists today. The term 'economic' was dropped in 1975, and the **European Union** was established in 1992.

The original EEC created a number of institutions. These included the **Commission**, the **Council of Ministers**, the European Assembly (which later became the **European Parliament**) and the **Court of Justice**. These ran parallel with the institutions of the ECSC and Euratom, until the **Merger Treaty** of 1965.

There were a series of debates as to how the EEC should evolve. Should there be greater **integration** between member states, or should there be wider membership? It could be argued that the EEC attempted to pursue both strategies at the same time. In doing so, the EEC did not really complete either of them fully. The EEC also suffered from national self-interest taking precedence over the interests of the Community. This can be seen not only in the **empty chair crisis**, but also where individual national leaders have scorned the intentions and actions of the EEC.

European Environment Agency   The European Environment Agency was established in 1990 and became operational in 1994. It was given a broad remit of helping to improve Europe's environment and encourage **sustainable development**. A wide range of areas is incorporated within the remit. Examples include air quality, noise pollution, water quality, wildlife (on land, in the air and under water), plant life and protection of the coastline. The European Environment Agency is an independent body whose membership goes beyond that of the **European Union** (EU). Currently there are 31 members, including all 27 EU **states**, as well as Iceland, Liechtenstein, Norway and Turkey.

In many respects, the European Environment Agency is a repository of information. It records, assesses and transmits data on the environment. The information is passed on to signatory states to aid them in improving and protecting the environment.

European Free Alliance   This **political grouping** within the **European Parliament** represents particular nationalities that do not have their own **state,** for example the Scottish Nationalist Party and Plaid Cymru from the United Kingdom and Esquerra Republicana de Catalunya from Spain. This grouping also represents disadvantaged minorities from across the **European Union.** It has been in existence for over 25 years.

The grouping is dedicated to promoting the rights of disadvantaged peoples across the EU. It is important to note, however, that the European Free Alliance is committed to using peaceful methods to achieve its goals. Environmental issues are also prominent in the European Free Alliance's agenda. This may be linked to regional environmental concerns being subsumed under national (state) interests, at the expense of the region.

The European Free Alliance sits in a group with the Green Party in the European Parliament. It is known as the **Group of the Greens/European Free Alliance.**

European Free Trade Association (EFTA)   This body was set up in 1960 as a direct competitor to the then **European Economic Community** (EEC). As its name suggests, EFTA was to be an organisation which promoted free trade rather than the setting up of a supranational body. The idea was to achieve total free trade in industrial products – as opposed to the emphasis upon agriculture in the EEC. Originally there were seven founder members (Austria, Denmark, Finland, Norway, Portugal, Sweden and the UK). They were known as the 'Outer Seven' as opposed to the 'Inner Six' of the EEC. This was a crude geographical distinction.

EFTA was not a great success – especially from the perspective of the UK. Most members have attempted to join the **European Union** at some time. However, the organisation still exists today. The current members are Iceland, Liechtenstein, Norway and Switzerland. EFTA negotiated special trading status with the EEC in 1972 which created a **free trade area** covering all EFTA and EEC (EU as it is today) countries.

European Liberal Democrat and Reform Group   see **Alliance of Liberals and Democrats for Europe**

European Monetary System (EMS)   The EMS was launched in 1979 in an attempt to reduce the wild currency fluctuations that had been occurring during the past decade. There had been earlier attempts such as the **snake in the tunnel** and the **Werner Plan**. Included in the EMS was the **Exchange Rate Mechanism** (ERM), as well as the introduction of the Ecu or European Currency Unit. The ERM, which was the most important part of the EMS, was about pegging national currencies to the Ecu within fixed bands of exchange (+/−2.25 per cent for most **state**s). The EMS was a system of (partially) fixed currency exchange rates between participating member states (in the early stages, the UK opted out). It was possible for member states to realign their currencies (that is, change band), although this was discouraged.

European Neighbourhood Policy (ENP)   The ENP focuses upon helping countries which are geographically close to Europe, and enabling them to benefit from the **European Union** (EU). It was first detailed in 2003. Due to their lack of economic (and political and social) development, these countries are unlikely to be able to join the EU in the near future. Rather than having such a divide across Europe, the ENP aims to reduce the gap in prosperity between EU members and non-members. Countries covered by the ENP include Algeria, Armenia, Azerbaijan, Belarus, Egypt, Jordan, Libya, Tunisia and the Ukraine.

European Ombudsman   The European Ombudsman was created in the **Treaty on European Union**. The post came into being in 1995. The current holder of the post is Professor Nikiforos Diamandouros, who has been in post since 2003. The post-holder is appointed by the **European Parliament**.

The idea of the **ombudsman** system is to help bring the **European Union** (EU) closer to the people. The Ombudsman investigates maladministration. Although this is a very difficult term to define, it is broadly to do with the way in which policies are implemented – in particular where policies have been implemented poorly or badly. It is not to do with whether a policy is good or bad but simply about the way in which the policy has been applied. Investigations can cover any part of the EU (except for the **Court of Justice** and the **Court of First Instance**), although it has been the **Commission** which has been most frequently investigated.

What makes the European Ombudsman an interesting body is that it can initiate its own enquiries. However, this must be to do with the EU. National concerns are beyond the remit of the European Ombudsman. This ability to start investigations gives the Ombudsman far more power than the Court of Justice, which must be asked to investigate any concerns within its remit. Decisions by the Ombudsman, particularly when proving maladministration, tend to be followed through and addressed. It is very rare for this not to occur. Should such a circumstance arise then the Ombudsman will write a special report to the European Parliament. This is the ultimate weapon of the Ombudsman. However, it is then left to the European Parliament to follow up the report. It becomes a political issue rather than an administrative one.

European Parliament   The European Parliament evolved from the Common Assembly of the **European Coal and Steel Community**. Originally, the delegates to this body were appointed from national parliaments. However, in 1979, **direct election**s were held for the first time. These are held every five years.

The European Parliament has been described as little more than a talk shop. In the early days, such a label was probably justified as it wielded few powers. Over time, the European Parliament has accrued more powers. The **Treaty on European Union** granted the European Parliament power of **co-decision**. In effect this means that the European Parliament must be consulted on any policy proposals and their suggested amendments given consideration. This forces the European Parliament and the **Council of Ministers** to negotiate over policy proposals.

The Treaty on European Union also gave the European Parliament the power of **assent** over **Commission** appointments. Thus, if the European Parliament refuses to accept the proposed Commission, new nominees must be found. Such a situation arose in 2005, when Commission president Jose Manuel **Barroso**'s nominees were rejected (ostensibly over the nomination of one candidate).

Finally, the European Parliament has power over the **budget** – sometimes known as the 'power of the purse'. The European Parliament has the power to reject the budgetary proposals of the Commission. This power was wielded frequently during the 1980s.

Representatives of the European Parliament are known

as MEPs (**Members of the European Parliament**). All MEPs are directly elected. However, the elections to the European Parliament are not held on a single day, nor are they held under a uniform electoral system across the **European Union**. In effect, these elections are often seen as little more than a plebiscite on the individual national governments.

When elected, the MEPs do not sit in national groupings. Rather they sit with like-minded thinkers (ideological trans-national groupings). Thus, there is the grouping of **European People's Party and European Democrats**, as well as the **Socialist Group in the European Parliament, Union for the Europe of Nations**, and the **Independence/Democracy Group**. Not all of the groups are fixed, as they change after some elections. The Independence/Democracy Group was formerly known as the Europe of Democracies and Diversities group. The current breakdown of groupings in the European Parliament is listed in Table E2.

Unlike national parliaments or assemblies, the

Table E2   Groupings and their MEPs (January 2007)

Grouping	Number of MEPs
Group of the European People's Party and European Democrats	277
Socialist Group in the European Parliament	218
Group of the Alliance of Liberals and Democrats for Europe	106
Union for the Europe of Nations Group	44
Group of the Greens/European Free Alliance	42
Confederal Group of the European United Left–Nordic Green Left	41
Independence/Democracy Group	23
Identity, Tradition and Sovereignty Group	20
Non-attached members	14

European Parliament is not a law maker. National parliaments or assemblies are known as **legislatures**. The European Parliament is unable to make laws but it is involved in the law-making process. The European Parliament is a co-decision-maker. It means that the European Parliament must be consulted in the legislative process. Failure to do so will leave legislation nul and void.

European People's Party and European Democrats (EPP-ED)
One of the ideological trans-national groupings within the **European Parliament**. It was originally known as the Christian Democrat Group when it formed to sit in the Common Assembly of the **European Coal and Steel Community** in 1953. It changed its name to the European People's Party in 1979 (after the first **direct election**s to the European Parliament), and became the EPP-ED in 1999. The EPP-ED covers the centre-right parties of the **European Union** – in particular the Christian Democrats of continental Europe and the British Conservative Party. In each of the elections to the European Parliament, the EPP-ED (or its predecessors) has been one of the two largest groupings within the Parliament – the other being the **Socialist Group in the European Parliament**.

Within the EPP-ED there is the European People's Party. This is the first trans-national European political party. Not all members of the EPP-ED belong to the European People's Party. One reason for this is that the European People's Party is broadly committed to **federalism**. Some members of the EPP-ED have reservations about this (in particular the British Conservatives). The EPP-ED is committed to greater **integration** within the EU but even some of its members are not wholly committed to such a position.

European Political Co-operation (EPC)   EPC was a precursor to the **Common Foreign and Security Policy**. It was formally introduced in 1970 and placed an emphasis on co-operation between member **states** in the area of foreign policy. The idea behind EPC was that the different member states would consult each other and the **European Parliament** on foreign policy matters.

European Rapid Reaction Force   After the war in Bosnia (1992–5), agreement was reached by the **European Union** (EU) at a summit in Helsinki in 1999 to establish a Rapid Reaction Force to assist in peacekeeping. The force was declared fully operational in December 2001. This came under the **European Security and Defence Policy**, which was part of the **Common Foreign and Security Policy**. It was hoped that the Rapid Reaction Force would comprise 60,000 troops, drawn from all EU **states**. However, there was to be no move towards creating some form of European army. Some member states, most notably Britain, did not want the Rapid Reaction Force to replace the **North Atlantic Treaty Organization** (NATO) as the cornerstone of European defence policy. The Rapid Reaction Force may only be deployed if NATO decides not to deploy any troops.

   The European Rapid Reaction Force is to respond to any of the **Petersberg Tasks** which were first detailed in the **West European Union**. The tasks cover crisis management, peacekeeping and humanitarian aid.

European Regional Development Fund (ERDF)   This is the largest of the **Structural Fund**s. The ERDF focuses upon developing and improving the infrastructure of regions across the **European Union**, as well as funding long-term job-creation schemes. It has been operational since 1975. The ERDF was established because of the regional disparities in development and wealth that existed across the **European Economic Community** (EEC) after the first **enlargement** in 1973. This applied to Britain and Ireland, but also included Italy. In Britain, the ERDF was seen as a means of correcting the imbalances in spending through the **Common Agricultural Policy** (CAP) where Britain lost out heavily to the rest of the EEC.

European Security and Defence Policy (ESDP)   This is part of the **Common Foreign and Security Policy** (CFSP). The **European Rapid Reaction Force** comes under this policy. It focuses not just on security and defence, but also on humanitarian aid and peacekeeping – sometimes collectively described as 'crisis management'.

One of the aims of ESDP is to work towards developing a Common Defence Policy for the **European Union** (EU). Such an aim was built into the draft **European constitution**. However, there is no objective of creating a European army. Rather, the ESDP functions alongside the **North Atlantic Treaty Organization**. What is also of note here is that despite disagreement over Iraq, the ESDP is still seen as a vital aspect of EU foreign policy.

European Social Fund   This is one of the **Structural Funds**, along with the **European Regional Development Fund**, the Guidance section of the **European Agricultural Guidance and Guarantee Fund** and aspects of the **Common Fisheries Policy**. The European Social Fund was established in 1960, although it was included in the **Treaty of Rome**. It aims to increase employment opportunities for all citizens across the **European Union**. The emphasis is not simply on cutting unemployment numbers in the short term, but rather on establishing job opportunities across the medium to long term. More recently, the emphasis has moved to combating youth unemployment, although this has not meant the exclusion of other employment issues such as adapting to technological change, or assisting migrant workers, the disabled and women. Between 2000 and 2006, around €60 billion was spent on European Social Fund projects.

European Social Policy   This was incorporated into the **Treaty of Amsterdam**. Prior to the Treaty of Amsterdam, there was an Agreement on social policy which had been established at the signing of the **Treaty on European Union**, where the UK negotiated an **opt-out** from this Social Charter. In the Treaty of Amsterdam, the UK renounced the opt-out.

The objectives of the European Social Policy focus upon conditions of employment, social protection and fighting social exclusion. This includes workers' rights in the workplace, for example working conditions and hours of employment. It also highlights what is termed social dialogue – this is where the **Commission** is required to consult with, for example, employers and trade unions on social and employment issues.

European System of Central Banks (ESCB)   The ESCB was first proposed in the **Delors Report** and came into effect on 1 June 1998. It covers all member **state**s, not just those participating in the **Euro**. Membership comprises the national central banks as well as the **European Central Bank**. The primary objective of the ESCB is to maintain price stability across all of the **European Union**.

European Union (EU)   The EU was established via the **Treaty on European Union**, signed at Maastricht in 1991. It extended the economic **integration** of the member **state**s, as well as their political integration, building upon what already existed via prior treaties such as the **Treaty**

of Rome. More powers were given to the EU institutions, especially the **European Parliament**.

Today, the EU is an economic superpower. It comprises a single market which covers 27 member states. This makes it a larger economic area than either Japan or the USA. As of yet, the EU has neither realised nor utilised the full extent of its economic might.

With this economic power, the EU is also developing into a global political power. The EU is probably the only power capable of standing up to the political might of the USA. However, where the EU is lacking in becoming a global superpower is in military might. Although the EU has established a **European Rapid Reaction Force** which comprises 60,000 troops, the reality is that, collectively, the members of the EU do not have the military capacity to challenge US hegemony.

Thus the EU is a group of countries which have developed common policies and common institutions to ensure peace across the continent. In this, the EU and its predecessors have been successful. There has been no military conflict between any member states to date. Although there is an ongoing process of integration, the individual members of the EU still retain their **sovereignty**. The EU is both **supranational** and **intergovernmental** in the way that it operates. It is a unique organisation.

European United Left   The European United Left organised itself into a grouping in 1989. Members of the European United Left come from non-Socialist left-wing parties across the **European Union**. These include Communist and former-Communist parties. It is a pro-European grouping, although there is some divergence of opinion between constituent members. For example, members are in favour of greater European **integration**, although there is disagreement over the best way forward. The European United Left is also committed to combating the **democratic deficit** that currently exists in the European Union.

The European United Left has allied itself with the **Nordic Green Left** to form a confederal group within the **European Parliament** which came into existence in 1998. Currently, the European United Left/Nordic Green Left has 41 **Members of the European Parliament**, including one from the UK (Bairbre de Brún of Sinn Féin).

Europeanisation   This is a rather complicated term. There are a number of different approaches and interpretations of the term. At the most basic of levels, it focuses upon becoming 'European'. The problem here is what is meant by the term 'European'. For ease of understanding, Europeanisation can be narrowed down to focus solely on the **European Union** (EU). Thus the idea of Europeanisation suggests that member **states** are being absorbed into this European organisation. This absorption can be forced, whereby the EU compels member states to act in a particular way, for example accepting the *acquis communautaire* upon joining the EU.

However, Europeanisation can also be seen in a less aggressive form. Europeanisation may focus upon sharing and possibly altering ideas and perceptions. This does not necessarily mean a top-down approach of the EU telling everyone what to do or think but rather a sharing of ideas to develop better understanding of people's positions on topical issues. Such a sharing of ideas may result in an understanding of why some people are anti-European or **Eurosceptic**, as much as why people are pro-European. In this context, Europeanisation does not necessarily mean imposing European ideas on everyone.

An alternative approach of Europeanisation focuses

upon the export of European forms of **governance** to non-EU states. Here, Europeanisation can be seen as the dissemination of good practice from the EU to the rest of the world. Such good practice could be institutional structures or the development of **common policy**. It could even be seen as a viable alternative set of practices to what is often espoused by the USA in the foreign policy arena.

Further reading: B. Rosamund, 'The Europeanization of British Politics', in P. Dunleavy et al. (eds), *Developments in British Politics* 7, Palgrave, 2003, pp. 39–59; J. Olsen, 'Europeanization', in M. Cini (ed.), *European Union Politics*, Oxford, 2003, pp. 333–48.

Europhile Someone who is enthusiastic about the **European Union** (EU). A Europhile is also likely to enthuse over European culture and society. While a Europhile may not be supportive of all policies or actions emanating from the EU, for the most part they are likely to be strongly supportive of the general moves towards greater **integration**. A Europhile is likely to believe that member **states** ought to cede **sovereignty** to the EU for the benefit of the greater good of all member states. However, not all Europhiles may necessarily support the idea of a superstate or the creation of a **United States of Europe**.

Similar terms to Europhile include pro-European, euro-enthusiast and euro-optimist.

europhobe This is a similar term to **eurosceptic**. A phobia is a fear, therefore a europhobe is someone who fears things European. In the context of the **European Union** (EU), a europhobe is likely to be opposed to membership of the organisation, and to encourage the withdrawal of their country from the organisation. The EU is seen to interfere in the everyday life of Europe's citizenry, while common policy such as the **Common Agricultural Policy** or the **Common Fisheries Policy** imposes unnecessary burdens on everyone.

euroscepticism   This is a catch-all term that is often used to describe people who are opposed to the **European Union**. At one level, this can be seen as an accurate observation. Eurosceptics, like anti-Europeans, are likely to encourage opposition to the EU, and to go as far as advocating **withdrawal** from the organisation.

However, euroscepticism can also be more about being a cautious or **reluctant European**. There may not be opposition to everything European. Rather, there may be scepticism or a cautious approach towards to the aims and objectives of specific policies or action. For example, being sceptical about the **Common Agricultural Policy** does not necessarily mean total opposition to the policy. Rather, a eurosceptic may advocate a radical overhaul of the policy, feeling that too much money has been misdirected and encouraged excessive **over-production** and that such a situation needs to be reversed. Similarly on the theme of **integration**, a eurosceptic may be opposed to the pace of integration rather than integration *per se*. The feeling might be that the EU is going too far and too fast down the path of integration.

Therefore, the idea of euroscepticism is sometimes misrepresented. Although the media may portray the term euroscepticism as being identical to anti-European, this is not necessarily the case. Eurosceptics may wish to slow the pace of movement towards the formation of a **United States of Europe**. They may even acknowledge that such a move will eventually occur. Their concern may be that in the rush to get to such an outcome, the means employed and their consequences may be detrimental to the EU and the member **states**.

euro-sclerosis   Euro-sclerosis is used to describe how not just the European economy has slowed down, but also the **integration** process. The term was used in the mid- to late-1970s to describe the stagnation in the process of integration within the **European Economic Community**, and again in the 1980s to describe how the economic growth of Europe had almost ground to a halt, while that of the USA and the Pacific Rim countries was accelerating.

The term has come back into vogue when comparing the growth rates of the **Euro**-zone countries to those of the USA. Since the introduction of the single currency, growth rates in the **European Union** have been very small, especially when compared to the USA or China. The accusation made against the EU is that its protectionist policies, along with the difficulties companies face in hiring and firing staff, has meant that levels of economic growth across Europe have been sluggish. In contrast, the USA has a far more flexible labour market (with relative ease in hiring and firing staff), and the US economy has benefited as a result.

ever closer union   In the **Treaty of Rome,** there is talk of establishing 'an ever closer union among the peoples of Europe'. Yet there was no specific explanation or interpretation of the phrase.

In the debate surrounding the **Treaty on European Union,** the British prime minister at the time, John Major, was fundamentally opposed to the use of the word 'federal' in the Treaty. In the UK, there was a fear that the term federal might be equated with a **United States of Europe**. Instead, Major argued for use of the phrase 'ever closer union'. However, there was some consternation among the other European **state**s as the phrase 'ever closer union' was believed to be similar to the concept of a superstate.

There is a degree of confusion over the phrase 'ever closer union'. It does imply the idea of the different members of the **European Union** working together more and more closely; of, ultimately, **integration**. The suggestion is that the different member states cede powers to a central authority, which is able to co-ordinate policies across all member states and to police them effectively, efficiently and fairly. John Major's perspective on this was that the member states would be able to refuse to cede powers in some areas, through the use of a national **veto**. Other countries were less sure of this. The feeling was that a federal structure would better protect national interests, rather than the idea of ever closer union.

It could be argued that the phrase 'ever closer union' does suggest the eventual creation of a United States of Europe. Of what it does not give any indication is when that might eventually occur.

Exchange Rate Mechanism (ERM)   The ERM was established as part of the **European Monetary System** (EMS) in 1979. The idea of the ERM was to create a degree of stability between the different European currencies. All currencies were pegged to the European Currency Unit (Ecu). The ERM allowed each currency to float by +/−2.25 per cent from their agreed peg. This was a similar approach to the '**snake in the tunnel**' that had previously been utilised. Not all member **states** joined the EMS – the UK decided to **opt out** in the beginning, joined at a later date, and was eventually kicked out of the EMS because the Government could not stick to its ERM peg against the Ecu. Italy was also ejected from the ERM at the same time, while the Greeks never participated in the ERM.

It was the general stability across all European currencies which had been created through the ERM that enabled Jacques **Delors** to introduce his plans for the establishment of a single currency.

F

federalism   This is a term that carries with it a lot of baggage, especially for **eurosceptics**. In the context of the **European Union,** the concept of federalism suggests the creation of a European superstate, modelled loosely upon the USA (which is a federal **state**). Other examples of federal states include Australia, Canada, Germany and Nigeria. From such a perspective, it follows that the UK will become no more than Texas (or any other state) within the USA, or Queensland within Australia. In other words, the UK will lose its **sovereignty**.

A federal structure involves the devolving of power from the centre to the regions. However, such devolution is protected by the **constitution**. Almost all federal states have a written constitution. The constitution will allocate powers to the different tiers of government. In the case of the USA, some powers are given to the states while others are retained by the federal government. Except in the most extreme of circumstances, one tier may not interfere with the operation of another tier. Added to this, neither tier of government is considered to be the superior: they co-exist.

The UK has been particularly resistant to the use of the word 'federal' in any of the EU treaties. Alternative terms have been utilised, such as **subsidiarity** and **ever closer union**. In each of these cases, it appears that some member states (most notably the UK) are a little resistant to the idea of greater **integration**.

When examining the EU, what currently exists is not a federal organisation. Rather, it is a **confederal**

74 THE EUROPEAN UNION A–Z

organisation. This suggests a far looser integration of member states.

federalist   see **federalism**

first pillar   This was part of the **Treaty on European Union**. It comprised the pre-existing communities, that is, the **European Coal and Steel Community**, the **European Economic Community** and the **European Atomic Energy Community**. The other two pillars concerned foreign and security policy, and justice and home affairs.

The emphasis of the first pillar is very much upon the Community or union. It highlights, for example, the role of the **Commission** as the only body which can introduce legislative proposals for consideration by the other institutions. The first pillar highlights the **supranational** aspects of the EU, while the other two pillars are more **intergovernmental**.

See also: **pillar of the European Union, second pillar, third pillar**

Fontainebleau Summit   This particular summit, held in 1984, is remembered as the one where the **British rebate** was agreed. Although that in itself is a noteworthy detail, far more was agreed at the Fontainebleau Summit.

In the early 1980s, the **European Community** (EC) was almost bankrupt. The **budget** was insufficient to meet all of the spending demands of the organisation. With Portugal and Spain expected to join the EC in 1986, there were likely to be even greater demands on the budget. At the Fontainebleau Summit, an attempt was made to resolve this situation. To finance the budget, the following measures were taken: an increase in **Value Added Tax** (VAT) contributions; limits on the growth of agricultural spending; and the introduction of **quota**s for milk production.

The increased VAT contributions meant that each member **state** was to pay 1.4 per cent of its VAT receipts to the EC. Previously it had been 1 per cent. Linked to this was an agreement to limit the growth of agricultural spending to prevent such spending from exceeding the EC's resources.

The British Government was fully supportive of these reforms. In fact, the British prime minister at that time, Margaret **Thatcher**, had been arguing for such reform. However, she was also of the opinion that the UK was paying far too much into the EC budget and that the UK required a rebate to achieve a degree of parity with the income received by other EC states. What was eventually agreed was the British rebate. This was about two-thirds of Britain's budgetary contributions. Since that time, this rebate has been a bone of contention among all member states.

fortress Europe   This accusation has been brought against the **European Union** (EU) for many years. It is all to do with trade, but is also linked to some of the common policies, particularly the **Common Agricultural Policy** (CAP).

Within the EU there is free trade between all member **state**s. The **single market** ensures that there are no internal **tariffs** to hinder the free movement of people, goods, services and so on. However, for non-EU members, there is no such liberal approach. Rather, there is a protectionist attitude. The 'fortress Europe' mentality makes it very difficult for non-EU states to trade with the EU in any goods that compete with a similar EU product.

Concerns about this fortress Europe mentality are not restricted to a few countries. Major trading states, such as Japan and the USA, have repeatedly expressed concerns over what they see as European protectionism.

More and more, developing countries are also voicing similar concerns. Policies such as the CAP, along with the idea of **community preference,** mean that it is very difficult to access the EU market with any product that competes with an EU equivalent. Even trade agreements such as **Cotonou** place restrictions on which goods may be traded with the EU.

The fortress Europe mentality also goes beyond trade. Non-EU persons may also find it difficult to enter the EU and to work in the EU. Such protectionism applies to EU jobs not just in trading issues (losing jobs to countries which can undercut EU products in price, for example China), but also employment issues.

founder member state   One of those countries which formed the original **European Coal and Steel Community** and the **European Economic Community**. The founder member **state**s were Belgium, France, Italy, Luxembourg, the Netherlands and West Germany. From the original six founder member states, after a series of **enlargement**s, there are now 27 member states.

Franco-German axis   This was sometimes known as the **Paris–Bonn axis** (possibly it should now be the Paris–Berlin axis). It describes the partnership between France and (West) Germany which has been the underpinning of the formation and much of the development of the different bodies, from the **European Coal and Steel Community** (ECSC) through to the **European Union** (EU). With the ECSC and the early days of the **European Economic Community**, it was French drive and German money that helped to establish the organisations, in particular with the roles of Konrad **Adenauer** and Charles **de Gaulle**. When there were only six member **state**s, these two countries dominated. Despite a number of **enlargement**s and a greater degree of **integration**, there is a feeling that they still dominate the EU. There was a hope among the other four founder members that British membership might reduce the influence of the Franco-German axis, but it was not to be. A lack of whole-hearted commitment from Britain meant that, for the most part, the axis remained unchallenged. If anything, it is the sheer volume of members that may now be challenging this axis.

free trade area   As the name suggests, a free trade area is a region where there are no barriers to trade. This could mean the free movement of goods, people, services and/or finances. However, there are different types of free trade area, depending upon the degree of **integration** between the **state**s involved.

A free trade area may also specify the ways in which participating states may trade with non-members. For example, ideas such as **community preference** may be applied. Such a move compels participating states to trade together rather than with a third party.

The **European Free Trade Association** (EFTA) was a free trade area. This organisation permitted the free trade of industrial products between member states. This type of free trade area saw very little integration between the participating states. The UK wanted no economic integration whatsoever. EFTA had a negligible overarching structure to monitor the organisation, with participating states meeting twice yearly. There are other free trade agreements such as the North American Free Trade Association (NAFTA) and Closer Economic Relations (CER) between Australia and New Zealand.

Another type of free trade area, which has a much greater degree of integration, is a **customs union**. This is what the **European Union** has become. This sees not only the free movement of goods, services and so on, but also the member states ceding powers to a central authority which then makes policy (in certain specified areas) on their behalf. It involves a degree of loss of **sovereignty**. A customs union also sees the introduction of a **common external tariff** and a **common commercial policy**.

functional   see **functionalism**

functionalism   This approach to **integration** highlights the importance of co-operation. However, a functionalist approach would focus upon developing co-operation in small, unimportant policy areas. It is far too difficult to get **state**s to work together on big issues without first developing some solid base of co-operation. Thus functionalism is incremental. Co-operation in one area will lead to co-operation elsewhere. This is often described as **spillover**. The idea is that co-operation in less important areas results in co-operation in other policy areas, without the participatory states being compelled to join in.

See also: **neo-functionalism**

G

Giscard d'Estaing, Valéry (1926–)   A former French president (1974–81), Giscard d'Estaing was asked to head the body which drew up the draft **European constitution**. As a centre-right politician, he established a new political party – the Union pour la Démocratie Français (UDF). He has a rather haughty, almost lordly, demeanour which does not endear him to everyone.

One of the reasons why Giscard d'Estaing was asked to draw up the **constitution** was his track record on the issue of Europe. Even before he became President of

France, he was a committed European. As president, he was an enthusiastic supporter of the creation of the **European Monetary System**. Giscard d'Estaing was also a key figure in moving the **European Parliament** towards becoming an elected body.

For these reasons, and many others, Giscard d'Estaing was seen as an appropriate choice to head the body which drew up the proposed European constitution. As a Frenchman, it was also felt that this would ensure French support for the constitution. Unfortunately, the French voted against the constitution in a **referendum**. Giscard d'Estaing has gone on record stating that the referendum result was a mistake that should be corrected. His work on the European constitution also resulted in Giscard d'Estaing receiving the **Charlemagne Award** (or Karlspreis) in 2003 for his contribution to the project of European **integration**.

governance   At one level, governance is about the different tiers of government feeding into each other. This could therefore mean the **European Union** interacting with central, regional or local government. Such interaction could be about the formulation of policy or policy implementation.

Yet governance can also include non-governmental bodies such as private businesses or voluntary organisations. All of these have a stake in both policy formulation and implementation. For example, a private company could collect refuse on behalf of the local council. The recycling policies of this private company will be influenced by decisions taken at the European level on environmental policy. Thus the private sector and at least two tiers of government (and central government is likely to be involved somewhere as well) are involved in refuse collection.

Greens   The Green Party in the **European Parliament** sits along with the **European Free Alliance**. While it is primarily seen as an 'environmental' party, it is far more. The Greens are also committed to a number of social issues, including equal opportunities, anti-racism and immigration. This is why the European Free Alliance may not seem as such an unusual bedfellow.

The Greens have **Members of the European Parliament** (MEPs) from a number of **European Union** countries: Austria, Belgium, France, Germany, Italy Luxembourg, the Netherlands, Spain and the UK. At this stage, there has been no breakthrough into Eastern Europe, although 1 MEP from Latvia, Tatjana Ždanoka, does sit in the **Group of the Greens/European Free Alliance**.

Group of the Greens/European Free Alliance   This **political grouping** in the **European Parliament** draws together two diverse groups of **Members of the European Parliament**. It comprises the **Greens**, who are committed to environmental issues, and the **European Free Alliance**, which is primarily concerned with promoting the rights of particular nations which do not have their own **state**. The grouping was created in 1999 and attempts to marry these two particular issues.

Arguably, each part of this grouping sees merits in the others' approach. Thus the European Free Alliance is committed to **sustainable development** and to working towards resolving environmental issues. The Greens argue that environmental issues should be fought at the European/international, national and regional/local levels.

Growth and Stability Pact   see **Stability and Growth Pact**

guardian of the treaties   This title is often used to describe one of the roles of the **Commission**. This role is detailed in the **Treaty of Rome**. It means that the Commission must make sure that all member **states** uphold the treaties of the organisation. Should a member state or even an organisation within the **European Union** (EU) be in breach of any of the treaties, the Commission may issue an **opinion** on the matter. Alternatively, the breach could be referred to the **Court of Justice**. A third option for the Commission is to fine the member state for the breach.

The phrase also applies to legislation beyond the treaties. The reality is that the Commission has to ensure that all EU legislation is properly implemented and enforced. To make sure that all of this can be carried out thoroughly, the Commission has a **right of initiative**. The possible penalties for any breaches are listed above.

H

Hard Ecu   Within the **Delors Plan** for the introduction of a single currency, the British Government put forward an alternative plan for stage 2. Rather than the proposed narrowing of fluctuations between currencies, the British Government proposed a parallel currency which would be tied to the value of the strongest European currency. This was to be known as the Hard Ecu. The Ecu (European Currency Unit) would be a parallel currency in all member **states**.

Very few countries expressed any interest in this alternative – only the Spanish appeared receptive to the plan. As a result, the idea of the Hard Ecu was dropped.

harmonisation   Developing common standards of production across member **states** of the **European Union**. The idea is to reconcile national differences and to create common rules. Such ideas are clearly part of the

integration agenda. This approach, however, has been slow and cumbersome, and is often perceived as being overly bureaucratic.

An alternative approach was the idea of mutual recognition. This was used as a means of achieving greater harmonisation. Within the **single market,** if a product could be sold legally in one member state, it could not be barred from sale in another. Thus the standards of production had to be recognised across the different member states. The only major exceptions to this could be made on the grounds of health and safety.

See also: **uniformity**

Heath, Edward (1916–2005)   Edward (Ted) Heath will be remembered as the British prime minister who led the UK into the **European Economic Community** (EEC), or **common market** as it was often known. **Europhiles** are likely to speak fondly of Heath's action, **eurosceptics** far less so.

Yet Heath's accomplishments should not be limited to merely leading Britain into the EEC. Much of his political career was intertwined with Europe. When Heath was first elected to the House of Commons, in 1950, his maiden speech was on European unity – and the need for Britain to engage with Europe. He spoke in favour of the **Schuman** Plan. In those days, however, Heath was something of a lone voice calling for British participation in Europe.

When Britain applied to join the EEC in 1961, Heath was given the task of chief negotiator. His performance in this role won admirers on both sides of the channel. He was, however, to be devastated by **de Gaulle** who vetoed the application in 1963. As some form of recompense, Heath was awarded the **Charlemagne Award** (or Karlspreis) in that year for his outstanding contribution to the process of European **integration**, that is, his attempt to get the UK into the EEC.

In 1965, Heath became leader of the Conservative Party. He was the first Conservative Party leader to be elected by party Members of Parliament. Although Heath lost the 1966 general election, he won the 1970 general election. Included in his party's 1970 manifesto was a commitment 'to negotiate terms of entry' into the EEC. Not only did the Heath Government negotiate terms of entry, it was also able to push the legislation through Parliament. This was despite the resignations of some junior ministers, as well as a party divided on the issue. It also required support from the opposition parties – particularly in the First Reading of the legislation. As a result, Britain joined the EEC on 1 January 1973.

Heath lost two general elections in 1974 and was replaced as party leader by Margaret **Thatcher** in 1975. Despite this, he still fought for a Yes vote in the British **referendum** on EEC membership in June 1975.

Throughout his career, Heath spoke passionately on the issue of Europe. He was particularly scathing about the way in which Margaret Thatcher treated Europe and the European project. Her actions, he felt, prevented Britain from participating fully in the **European Community**. In fact, Heath had nothing but contempt for any eurosceptic talk.

I

Identity, Tradition and Sovereignty Group   This is a far-right group within the **European Parliament** which came into being after the 2007 **enlargement**. The group includes the French National Front leader Jean-Marie Le Pen, as well as Alessandra Mussolini (granddaughter of the former

Fascist dictator of Italy). One British **Member of the European Parliament** (MEP), Ashley Mote, sits with the group. The group is led by the French MEP Bruno Gollnisch, who is under investigation in France for Holocaust denial.

The group is strongly **eurosceptic** and aims to defend Christian values, the family and European civilisation. It is also an anti-immigration group and opposed to any further enlargement of the **European Union**, especially the possibility of Turkish membership. This is somewhat ironic, as the existence of such a grouping was dependent upon the enlargement of the EU to include Bulgaria and Romania. While the group is portrayed in the media as an extreme right-wing organisation, members of the group dispute this perspective, claiming to be much closer to the mainstream of European politics.

immigration policy   The immigration policy of the **European Union** (EU) is somewhat complicated. Within the EU, there is supposed to be free movement of people across all member **states**. This was agreed in the **Treaty on European Union**. The reality, however, is somewhat different.

In the 1980s, the **Schengen Agreement** took the idea of the free movement of people within the then **European Community** much further. This covered issues such as visa requirements, asylum applications and a host of other immigration-related matters.

In 1999, at the Tampere Summit, there were calls for greater co-operation on the issue of immigration and asylum policy. There was a proposal for the development of a **common policy** on the issue of immigration and asylum. Added to this would be reinforced efforts to combat cross-border crime, but also rights for the victims of crime.

In 2003, it was suggested that the **Commission** establish a Border Management Agency. This body would work in tandem with national governments as the national governments retain responsibility for monitoring the external borders of the EU. Projects such as the **European Neighbourhood Policy** include within them policies on border management.

The 2004 **enlargement** of the EU saw a variable approach to the issue of immigration. The UK, Ireland and Sweden, in effect, had open borders for immigrants from the enlargement countries. All other members of the then EU-15 placed restrictions on immigration. Belgium, Finland, Greece and Luxembourg placed restrictions for two years. Germany and Italy, on the other hand, placed restrictions for up to seven years. In the 2007 enlargement, all of the EU-15 states placed restrictions on immigration from Bulgaria and Romania.

The draft **constitution** proposed the abolition of the national **veto** over immigration and asylum policy. This would leave it firmly in the hands of the Commission. As the draft constitution appears at present to be in limbo, proposals on immigration and asylum policy can be vetoed by any member state.

Independence/Democracy Group   This was formerly known as the **Europe of Democracies and Diversities** group. It is one of the ideological trans-national groupings (groups of like-minded thinkers) within the **European Parliament**. This particular grouping is seen as being rather **eurosceptic**. This euroscepticism is really the only thing that keeps the rather disparate parts of this grouping together. Most of the **Members of the European Parliament** from this group are British – although nine countries are represented in this grouping. Some specific political parties, such as the UK Independence Party, advocate their country's **withdrawal** from the **European Union**. Not all members of the group support such a perspective.

Prior to the formation of the **Identity, Tradition and Sovereignty Group**, the Independence/Democracy group was seen as being a rather right-wing grouping. This position has since moderated.

The ideas behind the Independence/Democracy group are to promote and protect national identities. The EU should be a group of **sovereign** states working together. The cultural traditions of each member state need to be protected to ensure that they are not subsumed into a giant European superstate. Proposals such as the draft **European constitution** should be resisted at all cost.

Instrument for Pre-Accession Assistance (IPA)   The IPA has taken over from the **PHARE Programme** as the major source of financial support for countries wishing to join the **European Union**. It runs from 2007 to 2013. The IPA is now the only financial assistance available for any applicant country to the EU, superseding all earlier projects. It is there to assist applicant **states** to reach the **Copenhagen criteria**. Upon joining the EU, IPA funding ceases immediately, although there is other support for new members of the EU.

Turkey has its own specific IPA agreement with the EU, as the Turkish application commenced prior to the introduction of IPA and Turkey was not technically eligible for PHARE funding.

Instrument for Structural Policies Pre-Accession   see **ISPA**

integration   Combining a range of different pieces into a single body, or the removal of barriers to enable the pieces to move closer together. Within the context of the **European Union**, this is where the different member states move closer and closer together, and may eventually become one.

The whole process of European integration – of bringing the member states closer together – has been something of a stop-start process. The major treaties, such as the **Treaty on European Union,** have given a huge boost to the integration process. The integration process is very much incremental. Each step towards **ever closer union** is built upon the earlier policies of the organisation.

There are a range of different approaches to integration, including **federalism, functionalism, neo-functionalism** and **spillover.**

intergovernmental   see **intergovernmentalism**

intergovernmentalism   The idea of the different governments of the **European Union** working together. There is no ceding of **sovereignty** to a higher body. Each member **state** remains sovereign and may well work to protect their national interests. An intergovernmental approach would see the different member states working together to achieve some form of compromise.

Intergovernmentalism is often seen as being the opposite of **integration.** Whereas the integration process of the EU brings the member states closer and closer together, the intergovernmental approach is somewhat resistant to that idea. Instead, the idea of intergovernmentalism is to promote the 'separateness' of each of the member states.

Yet there is a line of argument that sees intergovernmentalism as being an essential part of the integration process. This can be linked to the idea of **confederalism** or confederation. Through this approach, the individual member states retain their own importance. The emphasis is very much upon co-operation for mutual benefit.

Indirectly, the result of such an approach can be greater integration, but integration through co-operation rather than enforced integration.

IPA   see **Instrument for Pre-Accession Assistance**

ISPA   The Instrument for Structural Policies Pre-Accession, which was established in 2000 and ran until 2006. Sometimes it is known as the Pre-Accession Structural Instrument. It was created to complement the **PHARE Programme**, with an annual budget of just over €1 billion.

   The focus of ISPA was upon transport infrastructure and the environment. The funding was available for Central and East European states which were working towards the **Copenhagen criteria**. The largest recipients of ISPA funding were Poland and Romania.

   From 2007, the ISPA (along with all other pre-accession financial support) was superseded by the **Instrument for Pre-Accession Agreement** (IPA).

J

JHA   see **Justice and Home Affairs**

joint action   This is an aspect of the **Common Foreign and Security Policy**. Under instruction from the **Council of Ministers**, the member **states** are obliged to work together to achieve goals set by the Council.

Justice and Home Affairs (JHA)   This was the third **pillar of the European Union**. It covered policing and judicial matters, as well as **immigration** and asylum. At the **Treaty of Amsterdam**, this pillar was renamed **Police and**

Judicial Co-operation in Criminal Matters (PJCCM). At the same time, some of the features of this pillar appeared to be transferred to the **first pillar,** the Community pillar, for example the **Schengen Agreement**. The PJCCM pillar is still **intergovernmental** in nature and requires **unanimity** in all decision-making.

K

Karlspreis   see **Charlemagne Award**

Kohl, Helmut (1930–)   Helmut Kohl will be best remembered as the chancellor who, in 1990, reunified Germany. His contribution to the European process of **integration** was also quite profound.

Kohl became Chairman of the Christian Democratic Union (CDU) in 1973. In this post, he was effectively leader of the opposition until winning a vote of no confidence on the chancellorship of Helmut Schmidt. Kohl was Chancellor of West Germany (1982–90) and then Chancellor of the reunified Germany (1990–8). An interesting aspect of the reunification of Germany is that the former East Germany was able to enter the **European Community** without actually having to apply, or to meet any accession criteria.

Kohl was one of the driving forces behind the **Treaty on European Union** and also promoted **European Monetary Union**. His close relationship with the French President François **Mitterrand** enabled the development of a modern **Franco-German axis** upon which the **European Union** was based.

Kohl and Mitterrand were jointly awarded the **Charlemagne Award** (or Karlspreis) in 1988. The award is presented annually (normally to an individual) for outstanding contributions to the process of European integration.

L

legislature   Where laws are made. In most countries, the legislature is likely to be the nationally elected body. In the United Kingdom this is Parliament (of which the elected – and most powerful – component is the House of Commons); in the United States this is Congress (the House of Representatives and the Senate), although there is also a directly elected Executive in the form of the president.

In the **European Union**, however, this is something of a problem. The directly elected body is the **European Parliament**, but it is not a law-making body. Originally it could be argued that the **Council of Ministers** was the legislature. Laws were proposed by the **Commission** but needed the imprimatur of the Council of Ministers. Over time, this responsibility has been shared with the European Parliament, to the extent that both bodies are now **co-decision**-makers. However, unlike most legislatures, the European Parliament cannot initiate legislation.

Lomé Convention   The Lomé Convention (named after the capital city of Togo, where the convention was signed) was developed from the Yaoundé Convention. It broadened the **Yaoundé Agreement** to include developing countries from the British Commonwealth. The original Lomé agreement included 46 countries, all of them former colonies of the **European Economic Community** (EEC) member **states**.

In effect, the Lomé agreement was a combined trade and aid package for the signatory states. It was renewed and developed five times, with each package lasting for five years (although Lomé IV was technically a ten-year deal that had an extensive mid-term review which became known as Lomé IVb).

The content of the different Lomé agreements covered similar themes. These included financial aid packages for the signatory states, preferential trading status with the EEC/**European Union,** and guaranteed export earnings (a minimum price) for specific raw materials. Where there were goods in competition with EEC goods, access to the European markets for the Lomé signatories was far more restrictive.

The financial aid within the Lomé Convention focused primarily upon the development of infrastructure. This included roads, bridges, schools and hospitals.

The Lomé Convention was superseded by the **Cotonou Agreement** in 2000.

Luxembourg Compromise   A result of the **empty chair crisis** of 1965. There had been a dispute over the funding of the **Common Agricultural Policy** (CAP). The French Government, led by President **de Gaulle,** refused to accept the idea of the European Assembly (the forerunner of the **European Parliament**) and the **Commission** having the power to decide CAP funding.

The Luxembourg Compromise, which was eventually reached in 1966, worked on the idea of unanimous voting. Member states would attempt to work together to achieve **unanimity.** In effect, however, this gave each member state a **veto** over any policy proposals that might be considered to adversely affect their national interest. This veto could be used in the **Council of Ministers.**

M

Maastricht Treaty   see **Treaty on European Union**

Member of the European Parliament (MEP)   MEPs have been directly elected to the **European Parliament** since June 1979. The elections are held on fixed five-year terms.

Although the elections are held every five years, they are not really 'European' elections. Each member **state** holds its own 'national' elections for the European Parliament. Across the member states, there are different polling days and different electoral systems.

Although the MEPs are elected in 'national' elections to the European Parliament, they do not sit in national groupings. Rather, the MEPs sit in what are termed ideological trans-national groupings, or like-minded thinkers. The different groups include the **European People's Party and European Democrats**, the **Socialist Group**, and the **Union for the Europe of Nations**.

A key issue over the role of the MEPs is to do with how they are perceived. In the UK, for example, MEPs are often seen as failed national politicians. An MP who leaves Westminster to stand for the European Parliament is often perceived as a failing politician. Occasionally in the UK, people stand for election to the European Parliament and use it as a stepping stone to national politics, for example Nick Clegg and Chris Huhne of the Liberal Democrats. In other countries, such as Spain, successful national representatives are encouraged to stand for election to the European Parliament. MEPs are perceived to be 'superior' politicians to national representatives.

A broader issue linked to MEPs is whether they are national politicians or European politicians, both or neither. They are all elected in *national* elections, but to the *European* Parliament. The problem for most MEPs (although it could be argued for most elected politicians) is that they are not very well known within their constituency or within their country or across the EU. Their party label is more likely to be known – in fact within mainland Britain that is all that needs to be known as, in most cases, voters cast their ballots for a party list rather than individual representatives.

MEP   see **Member of the European Parliament**

Merger Treaty   The Merger Treaty was signed in 1965 and came into effect in 1967. It fused the different executives from the **European Coal and Steel Community**, the **European Economic Community** and the **European Atomic Energy Community**. This meant the formation of a single **Commission** and a single **Council of Ministers** for the organisation – as opposed to the three of each which had existed up until that point. The Merger Treaty also gave formal recognition to the role played by the **Committee of Permanent Representatives (COREPER)**.

Messina Conference   This conference took place in 1955. Its aim was to find a way of further developing the **European Coal and Steel Community** (ECSC). This included ideas such as the development of a **common market**. As a result of this conference, Paul-Henri **Spaak**, the Belgian Foreign Minister, was asked to prepare the ground for what would become the **European Economic Community** (EEC).

One interesting aspect of the Messina Conference was that the British Government was invited to attend. The six members of the ECSC felt it was essential to encourage British participation. The British response was far from enthusiastic. Two junior officials from the Foreign Office were sent in an observer capacity. Their report on the Messina Conference could be summarised as: if the EEC works, Britain might eventually have to join. This information was kept secret for 30 years.

Further reading: on the Messina Conference and Britain's role within it, see S. Burgess and G. Edwards, 'The Six Plus One: British policy-making and the question of European economic integration, 1955', *International Affairs*, vol. 64, no. 3 (1988), pp. 393–413

Mitterrand, François (1916–96) Along with **Helmut Kohl**, François Mitterrand is seen as being one of the political driving forces behind **European Monetary Union** (EMU), as well as many of the moves towards greater **integration** in the 1980s and 1990s. Mitterrand was one of the main architects of the **Treaty on European Union**.

Mitterrand became leader of the Socialists in 1971 and stood as presidential candidate in 1974, when he lost narrowly to Valéry **Giscard d'Estaing**. He won the next presidential elections and became President of France from 1981 to 1995. He was the first socialist president of the French Fifth Republic.

Along with Kohl, Mitterrand was jointly awarded the **Charlemagne Award** (or Karlspreis) in 1988. This award is given once each year, usually to an individual, for outstanding contributions to the cause of greater European integration.

Monnet, Jean (1888–1979) Jean Monnet is often seen as the founding father of the **European Union**. He was not a politician but rather an official. He drew up plans for a form of federal Europe during the interwar period. These were shelved but Monnet came to the forefront of the next European project after World War Two, influencing the then French Foreign Minister Robert **Schuman**. Monnet became the first President of the High Authority of the **European Coal and Steel Community** (the precursor to the current President of the **Commission**).

In 1953, Monnet was awarded the **Charlemagne Award** (or Karlspreis) for his outstanding contributions to the process of European **integration**. Schuman also received the award, in 1958.

Monnet was keen for Britain to be involved in the European project. However, he did note: 'There is one thing you British will never understand: an idea. And there is one thing you are supremely good at grasping: a hard fact. We will have to make Europe without you – but then you will come in and join us.' This was a profound observation, although the enthusiasm with which Britain joined the then **European Economic Community** (EEC) and its participation since did not live up to Monnet's hopes and dreams.

multi-layered Europe   With rising concern over the size of the **European Union** (EU) and how the **integration** process can develop, the idea of a multi-layered Europe has been put forward. At the first, or core, level there would be a highly integrated group of countries. The next layer would comprise those **states** that have joined the EU and who are working their way down the path of integration. Here can be seen a form of **multi-speed Europe**. The third layer comprises the countries that have yet to join the EU, but are likely to do so. These countries are likely to be focusing upon the *acquis communautaire*. The fourth layer includes countries in the **European Neighbourhood Policy**. This comprises countries which might aspire to joining the EU but are unlikely to meet the accession criteria for many years. The final layer includes everyone else who may at some time aspire to become part of the EU. The existence of this layer gives acknowledgement to the fact that the EU has obligations to much of a greater Europe – if not further afield. Europe may have a role to play in conflict resolution in the

Middle East, Chechnya and so on. Events that take place in countries which are, geographically at least, beyond Europe will still have an impact on Europe. It is very much the case that the EU needs to be prepared to respond to any such crisis.

Further reading: I. Kempe and W. van Meurs, 'Towards a multi-layered Europe', Centre for Applied Policy Research, http://www.cap-lmu.de/aktuell/positionen/2002/multilayered_europe.php, December 2002

multi-speed Europe   This approach focuses upon the problems surrounding greater **integration** within the **European Union** (EU). It has been suggested that, rather than forcing all member **state**s down the same integrationist path at the same speed, a uniform speed may not be the most appropriate method of enhancing the EU integration agenda. A multi-speed Europe envisages each member state progressing down the integrationist path at their own speed. A dual-speed Europe has been suggested which suggests a choice of two speeds: fast-track integration and slow-track integration. The multi-speed approach breaks this down even further. The end goal remains the same; it is merely the transitional period that remains flexible.

An example of multi-speed Europe in operation is with regard to joining the **Euro**. Originally, 11 member states signed up to the single currency. Greece succeeded in meeting the **convergence criteria**, but at a different pace to the original 11 members. With the **enlargement**s of 2004 and 2007, all of the new member states are expected to work towards meeting the convergence criteria to sign up to the Euro. Each of them is given leeway to work at their own pace. Slovenia has already succeeded in meeting the criteria and joined the Euro in 2007. Denmark, Sweden and the UK are also expected to work towards meeting the convergence criteria, but they have already negotiated an **opt-out** from joining the single currency.

N

nation   The terms nation and **state** are sometimes confused. Nations have objective and subjective characteristics. Objective characteristics may include a language, a common culture, a particular religion, a specific geographical territory, a national anthem and a flag. Subjective characteristics are to do with an individual's feeling for their nation or nationality.

Nationalism is about support for a nation or a national identity. At a basic level, nationalism can be seen in support for a nation's sports teams. Yet nationalism can also be linked to **xenophobia**, which is the fear of foreigners or people of a different nationality.

See also: **Union for Europe of the Nations**

national veto   see **veto**

NATO   see **North Atlantic Treaty Organization**

neo-functionalism   This concept is similar to that of **functionalism** in that it is working towards **federalism**, or at least greater **integration**. The approach, however, is somewhat different. Rather than focusing upon national actors, such as governments, the neo-functionalist approach also draws in non-**state** and sub-national actors. These could include pressure groups.

The neo-functionalist approach starts with economic links, such as business organisations and trade unions. Such groups have already developed links beyond the state and this compels the government to do the same. This is a form of **spillover**.

Spillover is a key concept in a neo-functionalist approach. Greater integration in one sector will lead to greater integration in others. For example, the integration of agricultural policies such as the **Common Agricultural Policy** (CAP) has led to greater integration in associated sectors, for example the environment.

An important point to note is that the neo-functionalist approach is to do with the process of integration. The end results may not work out as first planned.

Further reading: see Carsten Strøby Jensen, 'Neo-functionalism', in Michelle Cini (ed.), *European Union Politics*, Oxford University Press, 2003, pp. 80–92

Nice Treaty   see **Treaty of Nice**

Non-attached Member   A **Member of the European Parliament** (MEP) who is not attached or affiliated to any of the **political group**s within the **European Parliament**. The Non-attached Members are listed in Table N1.

Some Non-attached Members choose not to be attached to a political group as this gives them greater freedom to express their own ideas and beliefs, while other Non-attached Members, however, have simply not been welcomed into any of the groupings.

Nordic Green Left   A political grouping within the **European Parliament**. It has formed a **confederal** grouping with the **European United Left**. Collectively, both the Nordic Green Left and the European United Left are an umbrella for the non-socialist left-wing parties within the **European Union**.

The Nordic Green Left contains **Members of the European Parliament** from Denmark, Finland and Sweden. They are all part of the Nordic Green Left

Table N1   Non-attached Members of the European
Parliament (February 2007)

Name	Country	National party
Jim Allister	UK	Democratic Unionist Party
Peter Baco	Slovakia	Hnutie za demokratické Slovensko
Alessandro Battilocchio	Italy	Partito Socialista Nuovo PSI
Irena Belohorská	Slovakia	Hnutie za demokratické Slovensko
Jana Bobošíková	Czech Republic	Nezávislí
Sylwester Chruszcz	Poland	Liga Polskich Rodzin
Gianni de Michelis	Italy	Partito Socialista Nuovo PSI
Maciej Marian Giertych	Poland	Liga Polskich Rodzin
Roger Helmer	UK	Conservative and Unionist Party
Robert Kilroy-Silk	UK	UK Independence Party (UKIP)[a]
Sergej Kozlík	Slovakia	Hnutie za demokratické Slovensko
Hans-Peter Martin	Austria	Liste Dr Hans-Peter Martin – Für echte Kontrolle in Brüssel
Giovani Rivera	Italy	Uniti nell'Ulivo
Bernard Piotr Wojciechowski	Poland	Liga Polskich Rodzin

a. Kilroy-Silk left UKIP and set up a new party, Veritas, in February 2005.
He was, however, elected as a UKIP MEP and is listed as such.

Alliance (NGLA), which includes members from non-EU states – Norway and Iceland. The NGLA was established in 2004. Its underlying principles are egalitarian, but with the added emphasis on environmental issues such as **sustainable development**.

North Atlantic Treaty Organization (NATO)   A defence
pact signed by West European and North American **state**s
in 1949. The idea was to include the West German armed
forces within the treaty. The French were against such an
idea, and instead focused upon the **Pleven Plan** of a
European Defence Community. The European Defence
Community failed, and this left NATO.

The original idea behind NATO could be seen in the
Truman Doctrine of 1947. The aim of the Truman
Doctrine was to assist people who were fighting subjuga-
tion. The reality was that NATO was created to protect
Western Europe from a possible Soviet invasion. The
Soviets created their equivalent defence organisation,
known as the Warsaw Pact.

With the demise of the Soviet Union, many East
European states (former Warsaw Pact countries) have
joined NATO. This means that the role of NATO has
changed quite significantly. It is no longer merely a defence
pact. Rather, NATO now acts as an international police-
man and peace-keeper. The **European Union** has looked to
strengthen its role in these sorts of duties. As a result, it has
set up the **European Rapid Reaction Force**, which is to
work alongside NATO. This has caused some problems,
however, as not all EU members were in NATO. Some
states, most notably Ireland and Sweden, have a tradition
of neutrality and have never signed up to any defence
pacts. While they may be at least partially enthused about
a pseudo-European army in the guise of the Rapid
Reaction Force, links to NATO are seen as unpalatable.

O

ombudsman   This loosely translates as 'a grievance man'. The
ombudsman investigates maladministration – policies that

have been implemented badly, poorly or inappropriately. This can also include denial of access to information, discrimination, unjustifiable delays in obtaining information, or a lack of transparency. The system acknowledges that people need an avenue for complaint in such circumstances.

A **European Ombudsman** was established by the **Treaty on European Union** in 1992. The Ombudsman is appointed by the **European Parliament** after each election to that body. At time of writing, the holder of the position of European Ombudsman is Professor Nikiforos Diamandouros. He has held the post since 2003, and prior to this was the first national ombudsman of Greece.

The Ombudsman can receive complaints directly from any citizen within the EU or via a **Member of the European Parliament**. It is also possible for the Ombudsman to initiate an investigation into maladministration. This may be different to ombudsman system in the individual member **state**s. In the UK, for example, the Parliamentary Ombudsman (Parliamentary Commissioner for Administration) may not initiate any inquiries. The post-holder may only be approached by Members of Parliament, on behalf of their constituents. The Local Government Ombudsmen in the UK (there are several) may be approached directly by members of the public. There is no filter.

opinion Recommendations and opinions may be issued by the **Council of Ministers**. Both are purely advisory and are not binding in any way. Other **European Union** institutions may also issue their opinions on proposed legislation, for example the **Committee of Regions** and the **Economic and Social Committee**. There may even be an obligation to seek the opinion of such bodies. As with opinions issued by the Council of Ministers, however, they are not binding.

See also: **decision, directive** and **regulation**

opt-out   An opt-out can be negotiated by any member **state** with regard to a policy that may adversely affect national interests. Thus the UK, Denmark and Sweden 'opted out' of the **Euro**. Similarly over the **Schengen Agreement**, the UK, Denmark and Ireland were given opt-outs on a case-by-case basis. Arguably, with the application of the Schengen Agreement not being applied to all member states who joined in 2004 and 2007, every member state appears to have some form of an opt-out on **immigration**.

From the perspective of the **European Union**, however, opting out is perceived as an exemption for a particular member state. Thus, rather than a member state exercising their **veto** over a particular issue, the EU gives permission for that member not to be included in the policy. In this way, the EU can present itself as still being in control of the situation rather than individual member states holding the EU to ransom – as arguably occurred during the **empty chair crisis** in the 1960s.

over-fishing   There have been suggestions that fish stocks within **European Union** (EU) waters are being severely depleted. This has been a result of over-fishing the waters, that is, that too many fish have been caught. According to the **Commission**, which uses a sliding scale where 'over-fished' waters are not as bad as 'depleted' waters, limits need to be placed upon the amount of fish that can be caught. These limits are known as **Total Allowable Catches** and are part of the **Common Fisheries Policy**.

Part of the problem of over-fishing is that there is no agreement on how many fish are actually left. The Commission produces one set of results, estimating total fish stocks. As part of this, the Commission estimates that over two-thirds of EU waters are over-fished. The fishing industry produces a totally different set of results. In these figures, it is estimated that fish stocks are being replenished far more quickly than estimated by the Commission. Each claims that the other is inaccurate or that the estimates are flawed. Meanwhile, the apparent over-fishing of EU waters continues.

over-production   Quite simply, this is where too much of a product is being supplied. This has been most noticeable in the agricultural sector. With regard to the **Common Agricultural Policy** (CAP), over-production meant that more food was being produced than was actually required.

The original idea of the CAP was to maximise food production and agricultural productivity. There were food shortages in the immediate aftermath of World War Two and the founding fathers of the then **European Economic Community** planned to make sure that such shortages would never happen again, hence the introduction of the CAP.

In maximising food production, the CAP has been phenomenally successful – in fact, too successful. By paying farmers to maximise their production, the result has been that too much food has been produced, that is, overproduction. As a result, there have been a number of attempts to reform the CAP, including **decoupling** (which separated payments from production), introducing set-aside (where farmers 'rested' up to 17 per cent of their land, and were paid for doing so), and focusing more upon the 'Guidance' aspect of the **European Agricultural Guidance and Guarantee Fund** (EAGGF), with particular regard to restructuring the agricultural sector through such means as diversification.

All of these are different attempts to address the issue of over-production. At the same time, however, it is acknowledged that the EU still needs a farming industry. Thus there is a need for a balance between reducing production and enabling farming to remain financially viable, but without hitting customers' pockets and purses too hard.

P

Paris–Bonn axis   see **Franco-German axis**

Paris Treaty   see **Treaty of Paris**

Petersberg Tasks   With demands for Europe to play a greater role in crisis management, particularly from the USA, an agreement was reached at Petersberg (near Bonn) in 1992. At this meeting it was decided that the **West European Union** should play a greater role in a number of areas: peacekeeping; humanitarian aid and rescue tasks; and crisis management, including the use of combat forces in peacemaking.

The Petersberg Tasks were ultimately drawn into the **European Union**, when they were incorporated in the **Treaty of Amsterdam**. They have also become an integral part of the **European Security and Defence Policy**.

PHARE Programme   The PHARE Programme was introduced in 1989, and began operating from 1990. Originally, PHARE was an acronym for Assistance for Economic Reconstruction in Poland and Hungary. It was later broadened to include all countries within Central and Eastern Europe, including the USSR. With the break-up of the USSR, all of the newly created **state**s (such as Latvia and Lithuania) became eligible for PHARE funding. Poland and Hungary were the original targets as they were considered to be the most advanced, economically, in Eastern Europe.

The idea behind the PHARE Programme was to help during the transition from a centrally controlled economy to a free market economy. This would be a stepping stone towards applying for **European Union** membership. Thus the PHARE project can also be seen as a way of helping potential applicant states from Central and Eastern Europe achieve the *acquis communautaire*.

Between 2000 and 2006, €1.56 billion was made available each year for the PHARE Programme. At the same time, separate projects were also established to help in agricultural development (**SAPARD** – Special Accession Programme for Agricultural and Regional Development) and transport and the environment (**ISPA** – Instrument for Structural Policies Pre-Accession). Approximately one-third of the PHARE Programme monies was available for institution building, one-third for regulation, and one-third for economic and social cohesion. The money had to be requested by the applicant states.

From 2007, the PHARE Programme ceased to exist. It, along with the other financial support (SAPARD and ISPA) for Central and East European countries, was replaced by the **Instrument for Pre-Accession Assistance**.

pillar of the European Union   The **European Union** (EU) has three pillars. The **first pillar** is the Community pillar. The **second pillar** is **Common Foreign and Security Policy** (CFSP). The **third pillar** is **Justice and Home Affairs** – although it was renamed in the **Treaty of Amsterdam** as **Police and Judicial Co-operation in Criminal Matters** (PJCCM).

Most policies of the EU are covered in the Community pillar, including **European Monetary Union** and the

Schengen Agreement (although Schengen was originally part of the third pillar). The Community pillar is, by far, the most important pillar of the EU. Under it, only the **Commission** may put forward policy proposals. These are then considered by the **Council of Ministers** and the **European Parliament**. The Council of Ministers operates under **qualified majority voting** in areas under this pillar. The CFSP pillar covers foreign affairs, while the PJCCM pillar covers policing and judicial matters. Both of these latter pillars are, in effect, **intergovernmental** in nature. Decisions under both of these pillars are normally taken via **unanimity**, that is, member **state**s may have a **veto** over any policy proposals under these pillars.

One of the intentions of the draft **European constitution** was to merge the three pillars of the EU. Within this, however, there were to be special arrangements over particular issues of national sensitivity. These areas included foreign policy, security and defence. With the draft **constitution** currently in limbo, no changes have as yet been made.

Pleven Plan   The plan proposed by René **Pleven**, Prime Minister of France, in 1950 for the formation of a pseudo-European Army, under the moniker of the **European Defence Community** (EDC). The idea was to rebuild the West German military as part of the fight against communism, but not for it to be under German control. Rather, it would be under the control of the EDC, the institutions of which were to be modelled on those of the **European Coal and Steel Community**.

Pleven, René (1901–93)   As French Prime Minister, Pleven proposed the formation of the **European Defence Community**. His proposals became known as the **Pleven Plan**. Pleven was a centre-left politician who had far more in common with François **Mitterrand** than with Charles **de Gaulle**. Along with Mitterrand, Pleven co-founded the forerunner of the French Socialist Party.

Police and Judicial Co-operation in Criminal Matters (PJCCM)   The name for the third **pillar of the European Union**. This **third pillar** was originally known as **Justice and Home Affairs** (JHA) but the name was changed in the **Treaty of Amsterdam** in 1999.

Decision-making under PJCCM is normally taken through **unanimity**. It is very much an **intergovernmental** pillar, where each individual member **state** has particular needs and requirements that have to be met. Policy areas that come under this pillar include **immigration**, asylum, policing and criminal matters.

Some of the policies that were under this pillar (when it was the JHA pillar) were transferred to the **first pillar** (the Community pillar) as part of the Treaty of Amsterdam. This included the **Schengen Agreement**.

political group   While elections to the **European Parliament** are held at a national level, once elected the **Members of the European Parliament** (MEPs) do not sit in national blocs. Rather, they sit in political groups of like-minded thinkers. These are sometimes known as ideological trans-national groupings.

For a political grouping to be formed, it must comprise MEPs from at least five different member states. The largest political grouping in the European Parliament (at time of writing) is the **European People's Party and European Democrats** (EPP-ED). The different national parties that have signed up to the EPP-ED are listed in Table P1.

As a result of the size of some of the political groupings, they can best be described as an umbrella organisation

Table P1   Breakdown of parties aligned to the EPP-ED
(February 2007)

1. Демократи за Силна България/Democrats for a Strong Bulgaria (Bulgaria)
2. Alleanza Popolare – Unione Democratici per l'Europa (Italy)
3. Български Народен съюз/Bulgarian People's Union (Bulgaria)
4. Centre Démocrate Humaniste (Belgium)
5. Christen Democratisch Appèl (Netherlands)
6. Christen-Democratisch & Vlaams – Nieuw-Vlaamse Alliantie (Belgium)
7. Christlich Demokratische Union Deutschlands (Germany)
8. Christlich Soziale Partei (Belgium)
9. Christlich-Soziale Union in Bayern e.V. (Germany)
10. Coliga ao Força Portugal (Portugal)
11. Conservative and Unionist Party (UK)
12. Det Konservative Folkepartei (Denmark)
13. Dimokratikos Synagermos (Cyprus)
14. Erakond Isamaaliit (Pro Patria Union) (Estonia)
15. Evropští demokraté (Czech Republic)
16. Fidesz-Magyar Polgári Szövetség (Hungary)
17. Fine Gael Party (Ireland)
18. Forumul Democrat al Germanitor din România (Romania)
19. Forza Italia (Italy)
20. Gia tin Evropi (Cyprus)
21. Jaunais Iaiks (Latvia)
22. Kansallinen Kokoomus (Finland)
23. Křest'anská a demokratická unie – Československá strana lidová (Czech Republic)
24. Krest'anskodemokratické hnutie (Slovakia)
25. Kristdemokraterna (Sweden)
26. Magyar Demokrata Fórum (Hungary)
27. Moderata Samlinspartiet (Sweden)
28. Nea Dimokratia (Greece)
29. Nova Slovenija (Slovenia)
30. Občanská democratická strana (Czech Republic)

Table P1   (*continued*)

31. Обединени Демократични Сили/United Democratic Forces (Bulgaria)
32. Österreichische Volkspartei – Liste Ursula Stenzel (Austria)
33. Parti chrétien social (Luxembourg)
34. Partido Popular (Spain)
35. Partidul Democrat (Romania)
36. Partit Nazzjonalista (Malta)
37. Partito Pensionati (Italy)
38. Platforma Obywatelska (Poland)
39. Polskie Stronnictwo Ludowe (Poland)
40. Slovenská demokratická a krest'anská únia (Slovakia)
41. Slovenska demokratska stranka (Slovenia)
42. SNK sdruženi nezávislých a Evropští demokraté (Czech Republic)
43. Strana mad'arskej koalíicie – Magyar Koalíció Pórtja (Slovakia)
44. Südtiroler Volkspartei (Partito popolare sudtirolese) (Italy)
45. Tautas partija (Latvia)
46. Tèvynès sajunga (Lithuania)
47. Ulster Unionist Party (UK)
48. Unión del Pueblo Navarro (Spain)
49. Union pour un Mouvement Populaire (France)
50. Unione dei Democratici cristiani e dei Democratici di Centro (Italy)
51. Uniunea Democratä Maghiarä din România (Romania)

under which like-minded thinkers can operate. This does not mean to say that all MEPs within each political grouping necessarily agree on every issue. In fact, looking at the EEP-ED grouping, it seems rather unlikely that the Conservative and Unionist Party of the UK would sit in a grouping which is committed to **ever closer union,** if not a **federal** Europe.

See also: **Alliance of Liberals and Democrats for Europe, European United Left, Group of the Greens/European**

Free Alliance, Independence/Democracy Group, Identity, Tradition and Sovereignty Group, Non-attached Member, Socialist Group in the European Parliament, Union for Europe of the Nations

Pre-Accession Structural Instrument   see **ISPA**

Prodi, Romano (1939–)   Romano Prodi held the post of Prime Minister of Italy both before and after holding the post of President of the **Commission**. He held the presidential post from 1999 to 2004. Prodi's tenure in office was not seen as particularly strong. Like his immediate predecessor, Jacques **Santer**, Prodi lived in the shadow of the Presidency of Jacques **Delors**. What made Prodi's term in office even more problematic was that he failed to strike up a rapport with the leaders of the major **European Union** (EU) **state**s. This may have been to do with the fact that, ideologically, Prodi was left of centre, while President Chirac of France and Chancellor Schröder of Germany were right-of-centre politicians. Added to this, the Italian Prime Minister, the right-wing Silvio Berlusconi, appeared to conduct a feud with Prodi.

One major role that Prodi undertook with some vigour was the reform of the Commission. There had been much scandal and corruption under the Santer Commission and Prodi appeared determined to draw a line under such issues. Thus he strengthened the codes of conduct for individual commissioners, as well as reorganising the portfolios of the commissioners and those of the **Directorate**s-**General**. This transpired to be little more than a change in the veneer of the Commission. As a result, the Commission appeared to become even more cumbersome than it had been prior to the reforms.

Under Prodi's term in office, the EU officially started to use the **Euro**. Prodi is given some of the credit for this, simply for being President of the Commission when the currency was launched. The EU also experienced its biggest **enlargement** under Prodi, when ten countries joined in 2004.

Prodi was also key in broadening the idea of **governance** within the EU. It must be noted, however, that Prodi still saw the Commission as being central within the concept of governance.

A major criticism of Prodi was that he was determined to return to Italian politics after his term as President of the Commission. Thus there was always a feeling that his actions were taken to gain support within Italy rather than for the benefit of the EU.

Q

qualified majority voting (QMV)   This system is used for much decision-making in the **Council of Ministers**. Each member **state** is given a specified number of votes, dependent upon the population size of the country. Table C3 details the weights of votes for each member state.

From 1 January 2007, with the **enlargement** of the **European Union** (EU) to include Bulgaria and Romania, the weightings of QMV changed. Two conditions have to be met. The first is that a majority of members must support the motion (often it has to be two-thirds of member states). Second, 255 votes (out of the total of 345) have to support the motion (which is about 74 per cent of the total votes). Added to this, there could be a further requirement that the votes must represent at least 62 per cent of the EU population. Failure to do so would see the decision not being adopted.

There were proposals within the draft **European constitution** to reform the system of QMV, as well as to broaden the number of policy areas governed by this particular method of voting within the Council of Ministers. The proposal was to have a minimum of 55 per cent of member states (and 65 per cent of the EU population) to support a particular proposal for it to be accepted. For proposals to be blocked, at least four member states would need to vote against them. This would prevent the most populous states from blocking almost any legislation. Note that the largest four countries (Germany, UK, France and Italy) comprise over half of the EU population – collectively they make up 259 million out of the total EU population of 492 million, or 52.5 per cent of the EU population.

See also: **simple majority voting, unanimous decision-making**

---

quota   A limit or a restriction upon a particular product. The **European Union** is very keen to use quotas in a number of different policy areas. For example, there may be quotas on imports of particular products, or quotas on the volume of dairy products from a particular country and so on.

Quotas have been set as part of the **Common Fisheries Policy**. These are known as **Total Allowable Catches** and can be set by country as well as by individual boat.

The best-known quota has been set in the dairy industry, in an attempt to address the problem of **over-production**. Milk quotas were first introduced in 1983. They froze milk production at the 1981 level. Member states were each set a limit as to how much milk could be produced. This limit could be broken down to the individual farm level (with individual farmers being penalised for over-production), or to the level of dairies (with each dairy to be penalised for any over-production). In 1992, the system was simplified, with both dairies and individual farmers being penalised for any over-production.

R

Rapid Reaction Force   see **European Rapid Reaction Force.**

recommendation   Like **opinion**s, recommendations can be issued by the **Council of Ministers** but they are not binding in any way.

Recommendations are also issued by the European **Ombudsman**. These can be directed at any **European Union** institution. As the recommendations are non-binding, there is no obligation for the institution under investigation to address the issue or concern.

See also: **decision, directive, regulation**

red line   In any form of negotiation there are red lines. These are the points which are non-negotiable. There will be no compromise over them. If this cannot be achieved then the negotiations will be vetoed. With more and more countries joining the **European Union,** negotiations get trickier as every country has its own 'red line' issues.

In the negotiations on the **Treaty on European Union,** for example, the British Government had a prominent 'red line' issue. This was over the powers of the **European Parliament.** The position of the British Government was that any move to give the European Parliament legislative (law-making) powers was unacceptable. It was a red line. Should there be any move to cross this line then the British Government was willing to **veto** the whole treaty.

referendum   Where the people of a country are consulted on a particular issue rather than the elected politicians making the decision on behalf of the people. In such a manner, a referendum can be seen as a form of direct democracy – the people making the basic determining decisions. The use of elected representatives to make these decisions is known as representative or indirect democracy.

Many applicant countries have held a referendum on joining the **European Union** (EU) (or its predecessors). Member states have also held referendums on particular issues. The Irish, for example, are obligated by their **constitution** to hold a referendum on any European treaties. Details of the different referendums can be found in Table R1.

Referendum results have often caused problems for the EU. To use Ireland as an example again, a referendum was held on the **Treaty of Nice**. The Irish returned a 'No' vote. This result meant that the treaty was null and void, which, in turn, meant that the proposed **enlargement** of the EU to include countries from Eastern Europe could not go ahead. The **Commission** instructed the Irish Government to hold a second referendum and to get the correct result!

The French and the Dutch have both returned 'No' votes on the draft **European constitution**. This has been problematic for the EU. It may be possible to bully one small country into holding a second referendum – the Irish and the Danes have suffered such pressures. Two members returning 'No' votes, both **founder member states** and one of them one of the largest member states, has meant that the EU has had to put the draft constitution on hold.

Regional Development Fund see **European Regional Development Fund**

regional policy   European regional policy is aimed at reducing the disparities between the richest and poorest regions

Table R1   National referendums on European Union issues

Issue	State	Year	Yes (%)	No (%)	Turnout (%)
Membership	Ireland	1972	83	17	71
	Norway	1972	46	54	79
		1994	48	52	89
	Denmark	1972	63	36	90
	UK	1975	67	33	64
	Austria	1994	67	33	82
	Finland	1994	57	43	70
	Sweden	1994	53	47	83
	Czech Republic	2003	77	23	55
	Estonia	2003	67	33	63
	Hungary	2003	84	16	46
	Latvia	2003	68	32	73
	Lithuania	2003	91	9	63
	Malta	2003	54	46	91
	Poland	2003	76	22	59
	Slovakia	2003	93	7	52
	Slovenia	2003	90	10	60
Single European Act	Denmark	1986	56	44	75
	Ireland	1987	70	30	44
Treaty on European Union	Denmark	1992	48	52	43
		1993	57	43	86
	France	1992	51	49	70
	Ireland	1992	69	31	57
Treaty of Amsterdam	Denmark	1998	55	45	76
	Ireland	1998	62	38	56
Treaty of Nice	Ireland	2001	46	54	35
		2002	63	37	49
Euro	Denmark	2000	47	53	88
	Sweden	2003	43	57	83
Draft constitution	Spain	2005	77	23	42
	France	2005	45	55	69
	Netherlands	2005	38	62	62
	Luxembourg	2005	57	43	90

of the **European Union** (EU). It is not, however, a new policy. An emphasis on **regionalism** dates back to the formation of the **European Coal and Steel Community**, although the greatest step forward was taken with the formation of the **European Regional Development Fund** (ERDF) in 1975, followed by the establishment of the **Cohesion Fund** and the **Structural Fund**s (together with the ERDF are the **European Social Fund**, the Guidance aspect of the **European Agricultural Guidance and Guarantee Fund** and the equivalent in the **Common Fisheries Policy**).

The different regions of the EU are categorised according to their wealth (see Table S1). There is greater support for the least wealthy regions. The idea is to focus upon the cohesion of the EU collectively. To enable a greater degree of **integration** to occur, the extremes of disparities of wealth need to be addressed. To highlight the extent of the disparities with which the EU's regional policy has to contend, it is useful to examine the two extremes occurring in 2002. Although not in the EU at this time, the poorest region was Lubelskie (Poland) with a GDP per head of population at one-third of the EU average. The richest region was inner London, with 315 per cent of the EU average.

Arguably, there is a vested interest in the welfare of all EU partners. By assisting the least well-off regions, the wealthier regions may also benefit through, for example, greater trade. The problem is that with the last two **enlargement**s (in 2004 and 2007), the disparities between the richest and poorest regions have increased immensely. The EU may no longer be able to fund such generous support for Europe's poorer regions.

regionalism   This is sometimes seen as a response to globalisation but it predates the concept of globalisation by many years. As the name suggests, regionalism places an emphasis upon a particular region or regional identity. The **European Union** is probably the clearest example of such regional **integration**. There are, however, many other regional blocs, for example NAFTA (North Atlantic Free Trade Association), ASEAN (Association of South East Asian Nations) and CER (Closer Economic Relations – between Australia and New Zealand), to name but a few. These were all established prior to the widespread use of the concept of globalisation.

What has become apparent is that the importance placed upon regional identity has increased during the onset of globalisation. This is most obvious when examining the list of countries wishing to join the EU. Not only have 12 countries joined since 2004, but the list of countries expressing an interest in membership is also growing. It even includes countries which are, geographically at least, not part of Europe, such as Morroco.

See also: **federalism, fortress Europe** and **free trade area**

regulation   1. The most powerful ruling that can be issued by the **European Union**. Regulations have the direct force of law in *all* member **state**s and are binding in their entirety. Member states do not have to pass them in their own **legislature**s.

See also: **decision, directive, opinion, recommendation**

2. Regulatory bodies issue rulings on the areas within their ambit. These rulings are known as regulations. The **European Union** is an important regulatory body. It is the primary regulatory body in a number of areas, for example **Competition Policy**. In the transport sector, the EU has made it obligatory for each member state to establish a regulatory body for the railways. These bodies, in turn, can issue regulations – the rules under which the industry must operate.

reluctant European   Often used to describe the lack of British commitment to the **European Union**. Britain was considered a 'reluctant European' when it decided not to join the original **European Coal and Steel Community** when it was formed in 1951. Similar sentiment was expressed when Britain failed to join the **European Economic Community** (EEC) when it was first formed.

The problem here is with the idea of 'Europe'. If the issue were simply about membership, then Norway and Switzerland must be seen as being reluctant Europeans. The Norwegians were offered membership twice but the offer was refused through national **referendum** in 1972 and 1994. Therefore, with Britain joining the EEC in 1973, it might have been expected that the label reluctant European would be dropped. It was not to be the case.

When Britain did eventually join the EEC, the label remained because Britain did not appear committed to developing the European project. Renegotiating the terms of entry and then putting them to a national referendum highlighted a lack of commitment to Europe. This was exacerbated under the premiership of Margaret **Thatcher**, who was accused frequently of 'handbagging' her European colleagues. She demanded 'our money back'. The overall image that Thatcher gave to the **European Community** (EC) was of putting Britain's interests first and the EC's a distant second (at best).

Thatcher's immediate successors, John Major and Tony Blair, have both expressed a desire to put Britain at the heart of Europe. Their failure to do so, in particular through the use of **opt-out**s, has again highlighted a lack of commitment to the European project. Added to this, relating to the **budget**, is the endless defence of the **British rebate** or *cheque britannique*, which has caused innumerable problems within the EU. Hence the label 'reluctant European' remains.

What is surprising is that a number of other countries have displayed 'reluctance' over a number of different issues. For example, France and the Netherlands voted against the proposed **European constitution**. They are not the only countries to vote against EU proposals in national referendums (see Table R1). Added to this, the rates of implementation of EU legislation also show a number of countries with relatively poor records – and Britain is not at the bottom. With particular regard to the implementation of **directives**, Britain was ranked sixth in 2006, with Portugal languishing at the bottom of the 25 member **states**. Despite this, it appears to be only Britain that is worthy of the label 'reluctant European'.

right of initiative This belongs to the **Commission**. Effectively, it means that the Commission has the right to initiate any legislation. Such a right was underlined in the **Treaty of Rome**. It enables the Commission to fulfil its role as **guardian of the treaties**. The right of initiative was broadened, marginally, in the **Treaty on European Union** (EU) where the **European Parliament** may request that legislation be initiated by the Commission.

Although the Commission may initiate legislative proposals, these require the approval of other **European Union** bodies – the **Council of Ministers** and the European Parliament. Also, the Commission may not initiate legislative proposals in areas which are not EU **competences**.

S

Santer, Jacques (1937–) Former prime minister of Luxembourg, Santer was president of the **Commission** for one term (1995–9). He succeeded Jacques **Delors** and as such, great things were expected of him – especially in the light of the Delors legacy. The problem was that Santer had been a compromise choice for the post. Even he had not seemed overly enthused about his own nomination.

There had been strong support for the nomination of Jean-Luc Dehaene (prime minister of Belgium), in particular from the **Franco-German axis** of the **European Union**. The problem was that Dehaene was seen as too much of a federalist for the British Government, which led to the **veto** of Dehaene's nomination. Santer was seen as a more acceptable alternative to the British (and he was also, as a Francophile, acceptable to the French).

Santer adopted the slogan 'Doing less, but doing it better' for his Commission. This was something of a disaster. Santer wanted to focus upon better implementation of policies rather than setting up a major agenda of reform or greater **integration**. He was seen as a rather weak leader of the Commission. There were soon allegations of corruption against members of his Commission. This resulted in the mass resignation of the Commission.

Santer was a **Member of the European Parliament** (MEP) between 1975 and 1977 (when all MEPs were appointed from national **legislature**s rather than elected), where he sat with the **European People's Party** (EPP). After his stint as president of the Commission, Santer successfully stood for election as an MEP in Luxembourg in 1999, again with the EPP. He remained an MEP until 2004.

See also: **Cresson, Édith**

SAPARD   An acronym for Special Accession Programme for Agricultural and Rural Development. SAPARD was designed to help applicant countries prepare for the **Common Agricultural Policy**. The focus of SAPARD was on structural development of agriculture. This included the processing of agricultural products, improving veterinary control, diversification of rural activities, and the protection and conservation of rural heritage. The programme was designed to run between 2000 and 2006. It had an annual **budget** of around €0.5 billion. The largest beneficiaries of SAPARD funding have been Poland, Romania and Bulgaria.

After 2006, SAPARD ceased to exist. It was subsumed within the **Instrument for Pre-Accession Assistance**.

See also: **ISPA, PHARE Programme**

Schengen Agreement   This was signed in 1985 by the governments of Belgium, France, Luxembourg, the Netherlands and West Germany. The objective of this agreement was to enable the free movement of goods, services, capital and people across all signatory **states**. Thus border controls and customs formalities were abolished between the signatory states. At the same time, however, the Schengen Agreement aimed to tighten up border controls for entering the **European Community**.

The Schengen Agreement later became known as the Schengen Implementation Convention. It was extended to all member states of the **European Union** via the **Treaty of Amsterdam**. While, technically, there are now 30 signatories to the Schengen Agreement, not all member states have signed up to or implemented all aspects of the agreement. It is interesting to note that three non-EU states have signed up to the Schengen Agreement – Iceland, Norway and Switzerland.

The UK and Ireland have **opt-out**s, while Denmark has a partial opt-out. Ireland's opt-out is linked to an earlier agreement with the UK on the removal of border controls between the two countries. This would be rescinded if Ireland were to sign up fully to Schengen. The countries which joined in 2004 and 2007 are working to meet all of the Schengen *acquis*. During the Treaty of Amsterdam negotiations, one objective had been to make the Schengen Agreement part of the **first pillar** of the European Union. This was not feasible due to the opt-outs which had already been negotiated.

The Schengen Agreement aims to protect the external frontier of the EU. As a result of this, the Schengen Agreement has been to the fore of a number of related areas: asylum applications; the development of an EU visa; and law enforcement issues.

The introduction of the Schengen Visa, for example, meant that any non-EU citizens wishing to visit the EU could apply for a single visa covering all signatory states rather than having to apply for a visa for each individual state. Separate visas would still be required for non-Schengen states. The UK and Ireland have not signed up to the common visa, removal of border controls within the EU or the asylum applications.

Another feature of the Schengen Agreement was the establishment of the Schengen Information System. This enables the national police forces of all signatory states to share information more easily on a host of issues, most notably on 'undesirable elements' attempting to enter the EU. The UK and Ireland both refused to sign up to the information system. There was a feeling, particularly in the UK, that this would undermine national **sovereignty**. With the signing of the Treaty of Amsterdam, the UK and Ireland have agreed to join in on police co-operation.

Schuman, Robert (1896–1963)   As French Foreign Minister, Schuman unveiled the plans for the development of the **European Coal and Steel Community**, known as the Schuman Plan. Schuman provided the political impetus behind plans developed by Jean **Monnet**. The plan was for an incremental approach towards **integration**. As a result of his efforts, in 1958 Schuman was awarded the **Charlemagne Award** (or Karlspreis) for furthering the project of European integration.

The Schuman Plan proposed a pooling of resources – namely coal and steel – that were fundamental to fighting a war. By sharing **sovereignty** over these resources, it was hoped that wars between European powers (particularly France and Germany) could be prevented.

SEA   see **Single European Act**

second pillar   The second **pillar of the European Union** is part of the **Treaty on European Union**. It focuses on the **Common Foreign and Security Policy** (CFSP). This particular pillar is very much **intergovernmental,** as opposed to the **supranationalism** and **integration** which make up the **first pillar**. Like the **third pillar,** it is decided by the **Council of Ministers** rather than by the **Commission**. This means that it stays in the hands of the member **states** rather than being under the control of the **European Union** (EU).

The pillar operates by attempting to develop a **common position** and **joint action** on particular issues. Originally, this required **unanimity** in the Council of Ministers, although some changes were made in the **Treaty of Amsterdam**. These included the development of **common strategy** and the use of **qualified majority voting** in particular circumstances.

Despite the member states retaining 'control' over this pillar, there is an important point to note here. The development of the CFSP as the second pillar of the Treaty on European Union gave tacit acknowledgement to the role of the EU in foreign affairs. In earlier treaties, foreign policy was not even mentioned. It was clearly a national **competence**. The Treaty on European Union, through the formation of the second pillar, gave the EU a voice in both foreign policy and defence policy.

simple majority voting   A method of voting used in the **Council of Ministers**. It is employed for the least contentious of policies, such as procedural issues.

Within the Council of Ministers, each member **state** normally receives a set number of votes in relation to its population size (see Table C3). With simple majority voting, however, each member state gets a single vote. Currently, 14 votes out of the 27 are required to be cast in favour of a policy for it to be passed.

See also: **double majority voting, qualified majority voting, unanimous decision-making**

Single European Act (SEA)   This piece of legislation was proposed in 1985 by the president of the **Commission**, Jacques **Delors**. The SEA was signed in 1986 and came into force the following year. It gave greater impetus to the process of European **integration** and was, in many respects, the forerunner of the **Treaty on European Union**. The SEA created the largest **single market** in the world. When ratified, it covered the then 12 member **states**. It led to the formal creation of a European single market on 31 December 1992. In theory, this enabled the free movement of people, goods, services and capital between all member states. It was also decided in the SEA that all areas covering the development of the single market would be governed by **qualified majority voting**. A final point to note on the single market is that the SEA includes reference to the need for a further European treaty on any developments towards the establishment of a single currency.

The SEA gave new policy-making powers to the **European Community**. These were in areas previously not included in earlier treaties such as the **Treaty of Rome**. Some of the new areas included the environment and **regional policy**. Regional policy focused upon trying to reduce the disparities of wealth between the wealthiest regions and the poorest.

The SEA also enhanced **European Political Co-operation** (EPC). EPC covered foreign affairs. The SEA formalised EPC, enabling member states to work more closely not just on foreign affairs, but also defence and security matters.

There were changes to the European institutions as well. The **Court of First Instance**, for example, was established. New powers were also given to the **Council of Ministers** and the **European Parliament**. The **co-operation procedure** was introduced, which gave the European Parliament greater input into the decision-making processes.

single market   The idea of the single market is to treat the whole **European Union** (EU) (or **European Community** as it was known when the single market was first established) as if it were a single country. To this effect, there are supposed to be no internal frontiers within the EU. This should enable the free movement of people, goods, services and capital within the organisation.

By establishing a single market it was hoped that the EU would be able to compete better with the USA and Japan. Both countries had similar populations to that of the EU. The key difference was that prior to the establishment of the single market, the European countries were fragmented, that is, there were national frontiers between the member **states**, even though **common policy** was operating within all member states.

The legislation which promoted the development of the single market was the **Single European Act** (SEA).

This was proposed by the president of the **Commission**, Jacques **Delors**, in 1985, with the legislation passed in 1986. The single European market was in operation by 31 December 1992.

The problem has been that while a single market has been operating in theory, in practice it is not so clear. On the positive side, there are now no barriers for the movement of people, goods and services across most of the EU. There have been some restrictions with regard to the states which joined in the 2004 and 2007 **enlargements**. There are also issues surrounding the **Schengen Agreement**. Other positive aspects have been different European companies willing to work together, as well as an increase in the number of European mergers and acquisitions. The knock-on effect has been to enable the EU to compete with the USA and Japan in a number of markets.

On the negative side, there has been a lack of **harmonisation** in areas such as fiscal policy. For example, **Value Added Tax** (VAT) is not fully harmonised across all member states. There are different applications in different countries. There is an agreement to have a standard rate of VAT at 15 per cent or higher across the EU. Member states did have the right to have zero-rated products, that is, a rate of 0 per cent VAT on some products. For example, the UK has zero-rated products such as children's clothes, newspapers, educational texts and so on. Once VAT has been introduced on a formerly zero-rated product, it may not be rescinded. The bottom rate of VAT is 5 per cent.

snake in the tunnel   The term used to describe the system of fixed currencies proposed in the **Werner Plan**. A hoped-for consequence of this plan was to reduce speculation against the US dollar, as well as against the European currencies. The 'snake in the tunnel' commenced in 1972 but collapsed the following year as speculation continued against all of the currencies.

The currencies of the **European Economic Community** were pegged against the US dollar. There was, however, a margin of fluctuation of +/–2.25 per cent. The European currencies were, in effect, the snake. The margins of fluctuation against the US dollar were the tunnel.

Social Chapter (also Social Charter) The Social Charter from 1989, which became the basis for the Social Chapter in 1993 (in the **Treaty on European Union**). Although technically two separate documents, there is sufficient overlap between them to enable them to be assessed together.

Originally, the Social Charter was the Community Charter of the Fundamental Social Rights of Workers. This promoted a range of different rights for workers which formed the basis for the Social Chapter:

- Adequate remuneration for employment
- Collective bargaining
- Consultation and worker participation
- Equality of treatment, regardless of age, disability or gender
- Freedom of employment
- Health and safety protection in the workplace
- Social protection
- Vocational training

Unsurprisingly, the UK Government at that time was less than enthusiastic about such a charter. The UK Government under both Margaret **Thatcher** and John Major wanted a more liberal, free market approach to running the European economy rather than the social democracy model that was espoused by most other West European **states** at that time. The Major Government negotiated an **opt-out** from the Social Chapter of the Treaty on European Union. The argument here was that the Chapter would stifle economic growth, prevent the creation of new jobs and undermine the competitiveness of both the UK and Europe. This opposition remained until the Blair Government signed up to the Social Charter at the **Treaty of Amsterdam** in 1997.

The key rights for workers detailed in the Social Charter really represented a wish list. Much of it was also wide open to interpretation. For example, adequate remuneration for employment was interpreted as a minimum wage. The problem has been that the minimum wage is not uniform across the **European Union**. There are huge discrepancies between member states. As of January 2006, Latvia, for example had a minimum wage of €129 per month. In Luxembourg, it was €1,503 per month. The UK was set at €1,269 (£862) per month. All of these figures are pre-tax.

With the UK signing up to the Social Charter at Amsterdam, it ceased to be a Protocol of the Treaty on European Union. Instead, it became a full part of that treaty. Aspects of the Social Charter have been amended in both the Treaty of Amsterdam and the **Treaty of Nice**. The draft **European constitution** also contained some changes, but these have not been ratified.

Social Charter   see **Social Chapter**

Social Fund   see **European Social Fund**

Socialist Group in the European Parliament   This is the second largest grouping (and the largest left-wing grouping) in the **European Parliament**. It comprises social democratic parties from across the **European Union**.

Only Cyprus and Latvia do not have **Members of the European Parliament** sitting in this particular grouping.

One of the most important areas for the Socialist Group in the European Parliament is social policy. The Group places emphasis upon working towards a fairer society, and one that is more inclusive as well. In December 2006, the Socialist Group put forward ten principles for Europe's social future. These were:

- Rights and duties for all
- Full employment
- Investing in people
- Inclusive societies
- Universal childcare
- Equal rights for men and women
- Social dialogue
- Making diversity and integration our strength
- Sustainable societies
- An active Europe for people

(Source: Poul Nyrup Rasmussen and Jacques Delors, 'PES: The New Social Europe', 2007, http://www.pes.org/downloads/NSE_Web_interactive_EN.pdf)

Other areas in which the Socialist Group in the European Parliament is active include the environment, job creation and working towards a multi-lateral world order. This latter area sees the Socialists working with the Democrat Party in the USA on a host of initiatives, including nuclear non-proliferation and climate change.

sovereignty   The right of a **state** to pass laws within its own territory. This is sometimes known as internal sovereignty. There are suggestions that **European Union** (EU) membership undermines national sovereignty as all members have to cede a range of powers to the EU. Added to this, EU law overrides national law when the two conflict.

External sovereignty is when a state is recognised by other states as being sovereign. Such recognition legitimises a regime. The EU is seen as having such legitimacy in that it is able to negotiate on behalf of all member states where is has been given the **competence** to do so.

The concept of sovereignty is very emotive. Politicians such as Margaret **Thatcher** have made declarations that too much sovereignty has been surrendered to Europe. This appears to suggest that the **supranational** approach adopted by the EU is going too far and will lead to the creation of a **United States of Europe** or some other form of European superstate, and that it must be stopped. Charles **de Gaulle** appeared to have a similar perspective on Europe, as could be seen in the dispute which led to the **Luxembourg Compromise**.

The problem is that, as the EU is not technically a state, it does not have sovereignty, nor can it wield sovereign powers. It is merely an organisation in which the participants have chosen to enable supranational bodies to make decisions on their behalf. This could be seen as similar to a representative democracy where the representatives make decisions on behalf of their electors.

Spaak, Paul-Henri (1899–1972)   It was at the **Messina Conference** in 1955 that Paul-Henri Spaak was asked to prepare a report on the future development of European **integration**. Spaak, who was the Belgian Foreign Minister, was extremely enthused about the European project, and earned the nickname 'Mr Europe'. The Spaak Report, as it became known, outlined plans for the formation of the **European Economic Community** (EEC) and **European Atomic Energy Community**. This was the document which led to the **Treaty of Rome**. In 1957, Spaak was awarded the **Charlemagne Award** (or Karlspreis) for his outstanding contribution to European integration, that is, his work in establishing the EEC.

Spaak's involvement with the EEC did not end there. During the **empty chair crisis**, when the French (led by Charles **de Gaulle**) refused to participate in European matters, it was Spaak who played a key role in persuading the French to return to the negotiating table.

Special Accession Programme for Agricultural and Rural Development   see **SAPARD**

special relationship   A phrase used to describe the importance of the relationship between Britain and the USA. From a British perspective, it highlights that Britain, and British opinions, are considered to be of great importance to the most powerful country on this planet.

The close relationship between Britain and the USA, enhanced through a common language, has been highlighted by successive British Governments as the key underpinning of British foreign policy. This has led to accusations that Britain looks to the USA rather than the **European Union**. Some British Governments have perceived their role as a bridge between the USA and Europe.

The British applications to join the **European Economic Community** in the 1960s were blocked by President **de Gaulle** of France. He saw Britain as a Trojan Horse that would enable American culture and American ideas to pollute both France and Europe. From de Gaulle's perspective, the special relationship between Britain and the USA was a handicap for Britain. Britain was always willing to adopt the American position on almost any issue. Thus, during the Suez crisis of 1956, when the American Government questioned the actions of Britain, France and Israel in invading Egypt, it was Britain that backed down.

It must be noted, however, that the special relationship is not always about Britain aping US positions on various issues. The UK Government has, on occasion, stood up to the USA. An example of such an action was Harold Wilson refusing to send British troops into Vietnam in the 1960s. Although the relationship between Britain and the USA became somewhat strained at that time, the special relationship endured.

spillover   Spillover is a possible consequence of **supranationalism**. It is a key feature of **neo-functionalism**. A policy that is implemented in one area may have unseen consequences in another. Thus agricultural policy, for example, spills over into environmental policy. Arguably, as a result of spillover, almost all policy areas are now affected or influenced by the **European Union** (EU). Linked to this, spillover also helps to speed up the **integration** process.

Different types of spillover have been identified. The most widely known is **functional** spillover. As noted above, a policy in one area will have (potentially) unintended consequences in other policy areas. Political spillover is where a package of deals is made between the member **states**. This is a deliberate aim, unlike in the case of functional spillover. Finally, there is cultivated spillover. This is where the EU, or more specifically the **Commission**, attempts to establish an agenda that will push the member states further down an integrationist path.

Further reading: on spillover and its relationship with other concepts such as neo-functionalism and supranationalism, see Carsten Strøby Jensen, 'Neo-functionalism', in Michelle Cini (ed.), *European Union Politics*, Oxford University Press, 2003

Spinelli, Altiero (1907–86)   An Italian politician who had a vision of a **United States of Europe**. He felt that the agenda as laid out by Jean **Monnet** was doomed to failure. Monnet saw the need for an incrementalist approach, whereby participating **state**s would gradually cede powers to **supranational** institutions. Spinelli wanted a far more radical approach. He saw the need for a strong centre to set the agenda for the participating states. Strong European institutions were needed to counter the existence of strong national institutions.

Spinelli was nominated by the Italian Government for a post in the **Commission** in 1970. After six years in post, Spinelli resigned from the Commission to take a seat in the **European Parliament**. This was a major shock as in those days the European Parliament was little more than an unelected talking shop. The reality was far more significant. Spinelli saw the need for an elected European Parliament. He was merely positioning himself to become a dominant force in the European Parliament when such an event occurred (as it did in 1979).

After the first elections to the European Parliament, Spinelli started to campaign for a fundamental overhaul of the **Treaty of Rome**. He argued that, as a result of the **direct elections**, the European Parliament had a mandate to become a **legislature** rather than the talking shop that it had been. Spinelli's vision was still of a federal European state.

It was only with the **Treaty on European Union** and the European Parliament becoming a **co-decision-maker** that some of Spinelli's ideas began to reach fruition. It must be noted, however, that the **Council of Ministers** (and implicitly in this, the national governments of the member states) is still the dominant body in the **European Union**. Spinelli's concerns about Monnet's original plans for the **European Economic Community** and the programme of **integration** remain.

Stability and Growth Pact A key feature of **European Monetary Union**. The pact was agreed by all member states in 1996. It was engineered to stop states using fiscal policy (government spending) to get around the strict monetary policy requirements of joining the single currency. Two key features of the pact were that all member states would keep their **budget** deficits to less than 3 per cent of their GDP (gross domestic product), and that there would be an upper ceiling on national borrowing (60 per cent of GDP). Ideally, all participating states would try to work towards achieving a balanced budget. Any state which breached the pact could be fined by the **Commission**.

The problem has been that not only have the monetary policy requirements of the single currency been rather too strict, but so too has the Stability and Growth Pact. Around half of all member states which have signed up to the **Euro** have had problems meeting both the monetary policy requirements and those of the Stability and Growth Pact. France and Germany have both breached the requirements of the pact on more than one occasion.

state The **European Union** (EU) is often accused of aiming to become a European superstate. The problem with such an accusation is that questions must be raised about the extent to which the EU even resembles a state.

There are specific key features of a state, which are generally recognised among political commentators. The first of these is internationally recognised frontiers. While the EU is recognised as an international organisation, its frontiers change with each **enlargement**, or with the **withdrawal** of countries, for example Greenland, from the EU.

Within these frontiers, the EU has no control over law and order, or other related issues. There is no EU police force or army (even the **European Rapid Reaction Force** is not recognised as being a European army). While the **third pillar** of the EU is concerned with Justice and Home Affairs, the reality is that such areas are national **competences** rather than European ones.

There are other key features of a state. These can include a judiciary, a civil service or bureaucracy, a social security system and a government. While the EU may be involved in aspects of these areas (with the **Court of Justice**, the **Commission** and so on), the reality is that these powers tend to be retained by the member states.

Currently, there are 27 member states within the EU. A state has **sovereignty,** that is, the right to pass laws within its own territory. The member states, arguably, have decided to 'share' sovereignty with the EU, but only in specific policy areas.

Further reading: P. Dunleavy and B. O'Leary, *Theories of the State: The Politics of Liberal Democracy*, Macmillan, 1987

Structural Fund   Used by the **European Union** (EU) to develop **regional policy**. In particular, the Structural Funds are used to narrow some of the disparities between the richest and poorest regions of the EU. It has been noticeable with each **enlargement** that the gap between the richest regions and the poorest is growing.

There are a range of different Objectives of the Structural Funds. These are detailed in Table S1. In the period 2000–6, over €213 billion was spent on the Structural Funds.

There are four specific aspects: the **European Regional Development Fund** (ERDF); the **European Social Fund;** the **European Agricultural Guidance and Guarantee Fund;** and part of the **Common Fisheries Policy.**

Table S1   The Objectives of the Structural Funds

Objective 1: Structural adjustment of the least well-off regions
This takes around 70% of the Structural Fund budget. Regions under this Objective have a gross domestic product (GDP) of less than 75% of the EU average. Also under this objective are regions with very sparse populations, for example the northern regions of Finland and Sweden. Finally, Northern Ireland is also included under this Objective as part of the peace process in that region. All of the different aspects of the Structural Funds are utilised.

Objective 2: Development of regions facing decline
There are a range of different types of 'decline' under this Objective. They include industrial decline, rural/agricultural decline, urban regeneration, and decline in the fisheries sector. Approximately 11.5% of the EU is covered under this Objective.

Objective 3: Adaptation and modernisation of education, training and employment policies
All regions of the EU, excluding Objective 1 regions, are covered under this Objective. It receives just over 12% of the Structural Fund budget. Ultimately, this Objective is about training people to get them into the workplace. Objective 3 projects are funded exclusively via the European Social Fund.

The Structural Funds are not a substitute for national government spending. There needs to be a partnership between the EU and the member **state** receiving the funding. This is sometimes known as additionality, where the EU funds are in addition to national funding.

See also: **Cohesion Fund, regional policy**

subsidiarity   In relation to the **European Union** (EU), the person often credited with first using this term is John Major (UK Prime Minister 1991–7), during the negotiations on the **Treaty on European Union** (TEU). Major was fundamentally opposed to the use of the word 'federal' within the TEU. If such a word were used, he believed (and probably rightly), the British Parliament would refuse to ratify the Treaty. To resolve the situation, the term subsidiarity and the phrase 'ever closer union' were employed instead.

Subsidiarity effectively means devolving decision-making down to the most appropriate level of government. Within the context of the EU, this meant taking decision-making away from Brussels, and in particular the Commission, and handing it down to lower tiers of government. For Major, this meant giving decision-making powers back to the national capitals. Other members, however, viewed subsidiarity as providing the opportunity to devolve decision-making to sub-national government – at either regional or local levels. With the UK having a highly centralised system of government at that time, devolving decision-making to sub-national government was not seen as a viable option by the Major Government.

In the end, a full explanation of the concept subsidiarity was fudged. It was left to national governments to find the most appropriate level of decision-making. The Court of Justice was never asked to rule on an interpretation of the concept.

supranationalism The **European Union** (EU) operates through a combination of supranationalist and **intergovernmental** approaches. The **Commission** and the **European Parliament** are seen as supranational bodies. Their members are expected to think of themselves as 'European' rather than of their 'home' nationality.

The supranationalist aspects of the EU are where the member **states** in effect forgo their **sovereignty** – their right to make decisions in specific areas. These areas include agriculture, competition, fisheries and trade. This list of areas is expanding. Decisions made by the EU override those made by national governments whenever the two conflict.

Supranationalism is often perceived to be a stepping stone to the creation of a European superstate. In some countries there has been a backlash against supranationalism. Britain has been the most prominent member, earning the label '**reluctant European**'. However, the French and Dutch people both rejected the **European constitution** in national **referendum**s in 2005. One of the main reasons for such a rejection was creeping supranationalism – where the EU appears to be taking on more powers and setting more rules and **regulation**s without appearing to consult anyone.

sustainable development   This is one of the key principles of the **European Union**'s approach to environmental policy. Effectively, sustainable development is about how natural resources are used – that they should be replenished to ensure their availability for future generations. The idea is that while economic development is still considered to be necessary, environmental resources should not be exhausted in the process. Sustainable development is about leaving resources intact; about replenishing what is used. Added to this, sustainable development is also about cleaning up the environment, or at least attempting to repair the damage that has already been done to the environment – to the air, land and sea.

The problem with sustainable development is that it is seen as being eco-centric, that is, putting the environment first. This is actually a false assumption. Sustainable development is still anthropocentric – it puts humans first. There is still a push for economic development. As long as this happens, damage will be done to the environment. If a tree is felled, for example, it cannot be replaced immediately. It takes years for a tree to reach maturity. Even while the tree is growing, damage is being done to the eco-system.

T

TAC   see **Total Allowable Catch**

tariff   A form of taxation that can be placed upon any imported goods. Within the **European Union** (EU), with the establishment of the **single market,** there are now no barriers to trade between member **states.** There are no tariffs or duties on trade. The free movement of goods, services, capital and people is supposed to be the norm.

Externally, there is the **common external tariff.** Any goods entering the EU will have to pay a duty, regardless as to the port of entry. The duty should be the same in each member state.

The EU claims to be one of the biggest supporters of free trade, that is, trade without any tariffs or duties placed upon it. Despite this claim, there are accusations that the EU has a **fortress Europe** mentality, in that it tries to protect its home industries from external competition. This is carried out through the concept of **community preference,** as well as the use of tariffs on trade. Bodies such as the World Trade Organisation are supposed to encourage all countries to participate in tariff-free trade.

TEU   see **Treaty on European Union**

Thatcher, Margaret (1925–)   Margaret Thatcher was the first female prime minister of the UK. She held the reins of power from 1979 until 1990. During that time, she left a profound mark upon Europe. From her first meeting with other European leaders, where she demanded 'our money back', to the latter stages of her premiership where she expressed fears of 'identikit Europeans', Thatcher was seen as a profoundly **eurosceptic** leader. Yet the reality is not so clear-cut.

Thatcher had a vision of Europe and how it should develop. The problem was that her perspective was not the same as that of other prominent Europeans such as Jacques **Delors** (president of the **Commission** while Thatcher was prime minister), François **Mitterand** (president of France) and Helmut **Kohl** (chancellor of [West] Germany). It was definitely out of line with the ideas of Alto **Spinelli**. Thatcher saw Europe as a trading bloc, first and foremost. Ideas such as **integration** were to be avoided. Like the former French president Charles **de Gaulle**, Thatcher felt the need to put national self-interest ahead of that of Europe. As a result, Thatcher was sometimes described as a Tory Gaullist – a British Conservative whose attitudes to Europe were the same as those of de Gaulle.

In putting national interest to the forefront of any negotiations, Thatcher was able to stymie any progress towards greater integration. She successfully won the **British rebate** at the **Fontainebleau Summit** in 1984. Thatcher was also able to resist Jacques Delors' move to create a European **Social Charter**. The charter could go ahead, but with Britain choosing to **opt out**. This was where Thatcher expressed her fears of identikit Europeans – in a speech in Bruges in 1988. Each country working together (but as independent **states**), with their own traditions, customs and identities, was the way forward in Thatcher's eyes, rather than working to create some form of a **United States of Europe**.

Euro-enthusiasts could argue that Thatcher was the epitome of the **euro-sclerosis** that took place in the 1970s and 1980s. She was largely resistant to any fundamental change to the **European Community** if it was not in Britain's interests. Yet it could be argued that, in the longer term, this was of benefit to Europe. By slowing down the development of Europe, what did proceed was better thought out and implemented in a far better manner.

It was the issue of Europe which ended Thatcher's premiership. Her former Foreign Secretary, Sir Geoffrey Howe, condemned her attitudes towards Europe in a resignation speech to the House of Commons. This was the catalyst that pulled her from office.

Yet Thatcher's influence over European issues in Britain remained. She campaigned against the **Treaty on European Union,** even with the opt outs that her successor, John Major, had negotiated. Since then, Thatcher has also spoken out against the development of the single currency, against the development of a **European Rapid Reaction Force,** and against the draft **European constitution.** These are not seen to be in the interests of Britain, according to Thatcher. On the single currency, Thatcher sees any attempt to join it as an attempt to 'abolish Britain'.

Further reading: on Margaret Thatcher and Europe, see *One of Us*, Macmillan, 1989; *This Blessed Plot: Britain and Europe from Churchill to Blair*, Macmillan, 1999 – both by Hugo Young

third pillar The third **pillar of the European Union** is the third part of the **Treaty on European Union.** The **first pillar** covers the institutions of the **European Community,** while the **second pillar** covers foreign policy. The third pillar covers policing and judicial matters. This was amended in the **Treaty of Amsterdam,** with **Justice and Home Affairs** becoming **Police and Judicial Co-operation in Criminal Matters.**

The objective of this pillar is to develop **co-operation** between the member **states** in a range of areas. These include combating terrorism, racism, **xenophobia**, organised crime, illegal trade in arms, and corruption.

Decision-making under this pillar was to be **intergovernmental** in nature, rather than **supranational**. In this sense, it was the **Council of Ministers** which was to be the major decision-making body, not the **Commission**. The same applied to the second pillar of the treaty. With regard to the third pillar, the Commission was almost totally marginalised in this area. This may have been to do with the idea that home affairs was still a national **competence** rather than a European one.

Tindemans Report   Leo Tindemans, prime minister of Belgium between 1974 and 1978, wrote a report in 1975 outlining how the **European Economic Community** (EEC) could proceed down the path of greater **integration**. The problem was that Tindemans digressed from his terms of reference. Rather than outlining how to work towards a **federalist** Europe, Tindemans focused on institutional reform. He raised a number of concerns and proposed a range of developments. His proposals included extending the presidency of the **Council of Ministers** from a six-monthly rotation to a yearly rotation and subjecting more of the decision-making of this institution to majority voting. He also suggested that the **European Parliament** be directly elected by 1978. Tindemans also encouraged the development of a **two-speed Europe**, with countries moving along the path of integration at their own speed. On top of this, Tindemans proposed that more areas of **competence** be handed over to the EEC.

The reaction of the nine members of the EEC to the Tindemans Report was anything but enthusiastic. The idea of ceding more **sovereignty** to the EEC appalled both the British and the French. Even the idea of a two-speed Europe was met with concern. At the same time, the federalists within the EEC saw the Tindemans Report as being too incremental and lacking any drive towards greater integration. As a result, the Tindemans Report was, in effect, shelved.

Total Allowable Catch (TAC)   Part of the **Common Fisheries Policy**. Total Allowable Catches are set for each member **state** and cover national **quotas** for each type of fish or other marine life in each region of **European Union** (EU) fishing waters. One of the major problems surrounding TACs is allegations of their being abused. Fishermen in different countries have been accused of catching more fish than is permitted. Consequently, the TACs in these countries are reduced in the following year.

TACs are set each year. They are fiercely contested by all member states involved in coastal fishing around Europe. The UK fishing fleet (which makes up around 7.5 per cent of the EU fleet) catches around 10 per cent of all fish caught by EU boats. Of these, mackerel, herring, blue whiting and haddock are the most widely fished by British boats.

transparency   One of the key issues surrounding the **European Union** (EU) is the extent to which members of the public can see how the organisation operates. Linked to this have been accusations of a **democratic deficit**. It is difficult for members of the public to find out what is happening and to hold members of the EU to account for their actions.

The institution that is considered to be the most secretive is the **Council of Ministers**. Deliberations of the Council of Ministers are secret. Some of this may be attributed to national governments not wanting their citizens to know what has been sacrificed in the horse-trading that goes on in the EU. The problem here is that the Council of Ministers is an **intergovernmental** body. Finding out what goes on in their meetings may be slightly easier at the national level rather than at the European.

The reality is that there are two aspects to the issue of transparency. The first is the desire to know what is happening in the EU. In this area, the EU has been exceptionally good in creating greater opportunities to access EU documentation. It is the second area that is more problematic, and this is linked to the opportunity to influence decision-making in the EU. Access to EU decision-makers is not easy. Thus it is very difficult for members of the public to influence EU decision-making.

Treaty of Amsterdam   The Treaty of Amsterdam was signed in 1997 and came into effect in 1999. Its challenge was to make the **European Union** (EU) more relevant to its citizens, as well as rectifying some of the flaws in the **Treaty on European Union**. These grandiose aims were not, however, to be fully realised. The Treaty of Amsterdam highlighted the extent to which member **states** appeared reluctant to move down the route of further **integration**. It is very much an incrementalist treaty. The Treaty of Amsterdam develops and improves upon what already existed but without setting out any new agenda for Europe.

In trying to make the EU more relevant to its citizens, the Treaty of Amsterdam issued a degree of clarity on the idea of EU citizenship. While the Treaty on European Union established the idea of EU citizenship, the Treaty of Amsterdam offered a degree of clarity to this concept. In the Treaty of Amsterdam, the idea of EU citizenship is presented as being complementary to national citizenship, rather than replacing it. There had been fears expressed in some **eurosceptic** quarters that EU citizenship was replacing national identities. The Treaty on European Union had been a little vague on such detail. It was clarified in the Treaty of Amsterdam.

It was not just through clarity of the concept of citizenship that the Treaty of Amsterdam tried to make the EU more relevant. The treaty also reiterated the importance of two key concepts: **transparency** and **subsidiarity**. The perception was that the people of Europe did not know what was happening in the EU institutions. Greater transparency would enable them to see what was happening and provide greater opportunity to influence decision-making. Through increased use of subsidiarity, there would be more opportunity to influence decision-making at the levels of government below that of the EU. In these areas the Treaty of Amsterdam was not overly successful. Talk of greater transparency does not necessarily lead to it actually occurring.

In the Treaty of Amsterdam there was also a degree of institutional reform – although, arguably, it was little more than tinkering at the edges of the organisation. There was no major overhaul of the EU institutions. The powers of **co-decision** wielded by the **European Parliament** were extended into a range of policy areas. At the same time, more decision-making in the **Council of Ministers** was to be done through **qualified majority voting** (QMV).

The Treaty of Amsterdam also focused upon specific policy areas. The most important of these was in realigning aspects of the **pillars of the European Union**. Aspects of the **third pillar** (justice and home affairs) were transferred to the **first pillar**. This meant that they moved from the ambit of the Council of Ministers to that of the **Commission**. They became part of the **supranational** aspects of the EU rather than the **intergovernmental**. This also resulted in a change to the title of the third pillar. It became known as **Police and Judicial Co-operation in Criminal Matters** (PJCCM).

There was also a revision of the **Common Foreign and Security Policy** (CFSP), which was the **second pillar** of the EU. While the CFSP stayed intergovernmental in nature, steps were taken to make the policy more flexible. The idea was to move away from **unanimous decision-making**, but without introducing QMV. This was carried out with the introduction of **constructive abstention** whereby member states could abstain from a particular decision without utilising their **veto**.

Other policy changes in the Treaty of Amsterdam included environmental policy. The treaty drew in the concept of **sustainable development**. While this was something of a buzzword in ecological circles, there was a failure to explain the concept in the Treaty of Amsterdam. This was clearly a case of good intentions not being carried through.

A final point to note about the Treaty of Amsterdam is the incorporation of the **Schengen Agreement** into the treaty, but only as a protocol. This enabled member states with **opt-outs** in this policy area to retain them. Aspects of the Schengen Agreement could also be incorporated into national policy areas by the states with opt-outs, for example Britain and Ireland.

Treaty of Nice   This treaty was signed in 2001 but did not come into effect until 2003. While it was presented as being the treaty that would enable **enlargement** to the east to go ahead, the reality was that it attempted to tidy up a number of issues that should have been addressed in the **Treaty of Amsterdam**. These issues included institutional reform – something that was essential with the proposed enlargement to 27 member **states**.

The institutional reforms in the Treaty of Nice were quite extensive. The size of the **Commission** was evaluated. It was decided to reduce the number of commissioners for each of the larger states to one, where previously they had two. An upper limit was then set on the number of commissioners – at 26 – after any subsequent enlargements. At the same time, nothing was agreed on how the posts would be distributed among member states, except to state that it should be done in an equable manner.

There was a significant overhaul of the **Council of Ministers,** or, more accurately, the voting system used by the Council of Ministers. The number of areas subject to **qualified majority voting** (QMV) was extended. More importantly, the weightings of votes for each member state were re-evaluated (see Table C3) and the requirements to achieve QMV were also adjusted.

There were other institutional reforms in the Treaty of Nice. These included setting upper limits on the number of members in other institutions – most notably the **European Parliament,** where there was a proposed upper limit of 732 MEPs (**Members of the European Parliament**). With any future enlargements, some member states will see a reduction in the number of MEPs that represent them. Upper limits were also set on the number of representatives in the **Committee of Regions** and the **Economic and Social Committee.**

A key change was the introduction of the idea of **enhanced co-operation.** This took a degree of control over the **integration** agenda away from the Commission and into the hands of the member states. Thus member states could suggest ways in which greater integration of the **European Union** (EU) could proceed. Under enhanced co-operation, member states were not permitted to **veto** any proposals.

There were, however, major omissions from the Treaty of Nice. While there was an overview of the upper limits of representatives in the different institutions of the EU, no thought was given to the possibility of Turkish membership. If Turkey were to join the EU, it would have the same number of MEPs (and representatives in all the other institutions) and votes in the Council of Ministers as Germany. Currently, that would be 99 MEPs. With an upper limit set at 732, this would require a drastic overhaul of representation in the European Parliament. The same would apply to all other institutions, with the Commission likely to be the least affected.

A second omission was that the **Charter of Fundamental Rights** was not included in the treaty. It was approved at the negotiations but was left as non-binding on member states. There was an opportunity to develop this document along the lines of a bill of rights for all citizens within the EU. National self-interest, among other things, prevented any great strides forward in this area of citizens' rights.

A final point to note about the Treaty of Nice is that it almost failed to proceed. According to the Irish **constitution**, any major treaties have to be subject to a national **referendum**. When the Irish held their referendum, the treaty was defeated. The reason for the defeat was that, among others, the agricultural lobby highlighted how much less revenue Ireland would receive from the EU (and particularly the **Common Agricultural Policy**) if the Eastern European states were to join. After the referendum, the Commission ordered the Irish Government to hold a second referendum and to get the 'right' result (see Table R1).

Treaty of Paris   The origins of the Treaty of Paris were in the **Schuman** Plan. The development of this plan led to the treaty becoming the founding document of the **European Coal and Steel Community** (ECSC). It was signed in 1951 and came into effect the following year. Under the treaty, the ECSC had an agreed lifespan of 50 years. Thus, in 2002, the ECSC ceased to exist.

The idea was that this organisation would work towards greater prosperity for all member **states** through the pooling of economic resources – or at least those linked to coal and steel. Linked to this would be the development of a **single market** for these resources.

The Treaty of Paris provided for a number of institutions to monitor the operations of the ECSC. These were: a High Authority (the precursor to the **Commission**), whose first head was Jean **Monnet**; a Special **Council of Ministers** which covered national representation; a nominated assembly from representatives of national assemblies (although there were demands that the assembly of the ECSC should be directly elected); and a **Court of Justice**.

Treaty of Rome   The founding document of the **European Economic Community** (EEC) was the Treaty of Rome. Its origins were in the **Messina Conference** and the **Spaak** Report. There was also a second Treaty of Rome which established the **European Atomic Energy Community**. Both were signed in 1957 and came into effect the following year. The original signatory **states** were Belgium, France, Italy, Luxembourg, the Netherlands and West Germany.

While the origins of the Treaty of Rome can also be seen in the development of the **European Coal and Steel Community** (ECSC) and the **Treaty of Paris**, any **supranational** ideas were not that straightforward. The **European Defence Community** had been a failure and there were feelings that the ECSC may also be doomed to failure. Thus the idea of integrating national economies had to be done incrementally, and with the support of all member states.

The founding idea behind the Treaty of Rome was to establish an 'ever closer union among the peoples of Europe'. The way forward was through economic integration. The Treaty of Rome aimed to create a customs union and then a common market within 12 years. This was an ambitious plan. It was not realised to the original timescale, but both aims were eventually achieved after the Single European Act (SEA) and the Treaty on European Union.

Many of the aims of the EEC were similar to those of the ECSC. This is hardly surprising as, if it were not for the ECSC being in existence, then it would have been most unlikely that the EEC would have been formed. On top of this, the institutions of the EEC were also modelled on those of the ECSC: a Commission; a Council of Ministers; an appointed assembly (which later became the European Parliament); and a Court of Justice. Added to these was the establishment of the Court of Auditors and the Committee of Permanent Representatives.

A range of policy issues were also covered in the Treaty of Rome for the EEC. There was the proposed introduction of common policy in agriculture, fisheries and transport, the establishment of the European Social Fund, the development of a common external tariff, and the introduction of a Competition Policy. Added to this, there were trade agreements with former colonies. This was the forerunner to the Yaoundé Agreement.

Treaty on European Union (TEU)   This treaty is sometimes known as the Maastricht Treaty, after the name of the town where the treaty was signed. It was one of the most significant treaties to have been signed by the participating

European **states**. The basis for this treaty came from the **Single European Act** which had been signed in 1986.

The TEU contained both policy changes and institutional changes. The institutional changes saw the establishment of a number of new bodies: the **Committee of Regions**, the **European Central Bank** and the **European Ombudsman**. Added to this, the **Court of Auditors** was upgraded to an institution.

There were also changes to the **European Parliament** and its role in the legislative processes of the **European Union** (EU). The European Parliament was given the power of **co-decision**, to be shared with the **Council of Ministers**. This gave the European Parliament a much firmer standing in the legislative processes of the EU, although it was still unable to initiate legislation.

The final institutional change was probably more constitutional in nature. The three **pillars of the European Union** were introduced. The **first pillar** comprised the **European Community** and all of the institutions that already existed. The **second pillar** was related to foreign and security policy. The **third pillar** focused upon justice and home affairs.

The policy changes within the organisation were varied, although in some cases member states negotiated **opt-outs** from particular areas. The most significant policy change was the timetabling of **Economic and Monetary Union**. This had been detailed in the **Delors Report** but no timetable had been devised. Jacques **Delors** merely outlined the stages involved (see Table D1) (and Denmark and the UK chose to opt out of the final stage, which was the launch of the **Euro**). Included in this timetable were the **convergence criteria**. These detailed how the different European currencies were to be brought together.

Other policy changes saw the EU gain **competence** in a number of areas. These included education, public health, consumer protection and social policy. This latter area was problematic as the UK opted out of the **Social Chapter**. As a result, there was a protocol on social policy at the end of the treaty. This has since been repealed, when the UK signed up to the Social Charter in the **Treaty of Amsterdam**.

The establishment of the **Common Foreign and Security Policy** as part of the second pillar of the TEU saw the EU gain a foothold in one of the most problematic policy areas. The member states jealously guarded their foreign and defence policies from European interference. Yet the establishment of this second pillar, even though it was **intergovernmental** and under the auspices of the Council of Ministers, saw the EU take a step forward in foreign and defence policy beyond what had been established under **European Political Co-operation**.

The TEU also established the idea of a European citizenship. This meant, for example, that citizens of the EU would carry European passports rather than national ones. In some **eurosceptic** quarters, this was seen as the EU trying to phase out national identities as part of a process that would see the establishment of a European state. This issue was cleared up in the Treaty of Amsterdam where it was stated that EU citizenship complemented national citizenship rather than replaced it.

A final area of note is the introduction of the term **subsidiarity**. The advocate of such a term was the British prime minister John Major. He saw the use of this concept as a means of taking some decision-making away from the EU and returning it to national governments. Similarly, Major was also the extoller of the phrase '**ever closer union**' which is used in the treaty rather than the term '**federal**'. Major felt that if the term federal were in the treaty then the document would not be ratified in the British Parliament.

Once the treaty had been signed, it needed to be ratified in all member states. Here there was a snag. The Danes held a **referendum** and returned a 'No' vote (see Table R1). Eurosceptics across Europe argued that the treaty was dead. The **Commission**, on the other hand, ordered the Danes to hold a second referendum after some alterations to the treaty had been made.

two-speed Europe   This approach is where different parts of the **European Union** integrate at different rates: a fast track of deeper **integration** and a slow track of more gradual integration. Arguably, there could be a **multi-speed Europe**.

The idea of a two-speed Europe had been suggested in the **Tindemans Report**. At that time, the idea was met with a great deal of resistance. Yet a two-speed, or even a multi-speed, Europe already exists today. As member states meet the **convergence criteria** to join the **Euro**, they are able to join. Thus Slovenia was able to join the Eurozone in January 2007. None of the other accession countries of 2004 are anywhere near to meeting the criteria. As they do so, they will join.

Formally, there is no two-speed Europe. The idea of a fast track to integration and a slow track, running parallel with each other, would still be met with much resistance. Those on the slower track may be perceived as being less enthused or less committed to the European project, regardless as to whether or not that it is the case.

U

UEN   see **Union for Europe of the Nations**

unanimity   see **unanimous decision-making**

unanimous decision-making   Unanimous decision-making, or unanimity, was a result of the **Luxembourg Compromise**. In effect, it means that all member **state**s must be in support of a policy proposal in the **Council of Ministers** for it to go ahead.

There was a reduction in the number of decisions subject to unanimity as a result of the **Single European Act**. After that particular piece of legislation, many more decisions became subject to **qualified majority voting** (QMV). The number of areas which are now subject to QMV has grown. There are, however, specific areas where unanimity is still required. One of the most prominent of these is **enlargement**. For a new member to accede to the **European Union**, all member states must be in support. An example of where unanimous support did not occur is the **Treaty of Nice**. The Irish had to subject this treaty to a national **referendum**. It was defeated, which meant that the proposed enlargement of 2004 could not proceed. A second referendum was held at a later date which enabled the enlargement to go ahead.

uniform electoral procedure   The first **direct election**s to the **European Parliament** were held in 1979. At that time, each member **state** could choose which electoral system it wished to use. This resulted in a multiplicity of electoral systems being used.

There have been a number of attempts to introduce a degree of **harmonisation** of electoral systems used in elections to the European Parliament. Since 1999, all states have used some form of proportional representation (PR), with the UK moving into line with everyone else. Although PR is used by all member states, there is still no uniform electoral procedure. Voting days are different. Even the forms of PR are different. Some member states use national party lists (for example, the Netherlands and

Spain) while others use regional lists (for example, Ireland and the UK). France moved from a national list to regional lists for the 2004 elections.

The Adonnino Committee, which was established in 1984, suggested that a uniform electoral procedure would help the **European Community** to better engage with European citizens. This was not the first time that such a proposal had been raised – it was even mentioned in the **Treaty of Rome**. The **European Union** is yet to act on such a proposal.

Further reading: A. Jones, 'European Union Electoral Systems – An Overview of the Electoral Systems of the European Parliament and the National Legislatures', *Talking Politics*, vol. 6, no. 3, May 1994

uniformity   The idea of uniformity in the **European Union** (EU) suggests that the same basic rules ought to apply across all member **state**s. There should be uniformity in practice. This does not mean making everything the same in all member states. Rather, that there should be similar basic standards in all practices. Thus, for example, when looking at the reform of the **Common Agricultural Policy**, there should be uniform standards of food safety across all member states. This does not mean that all food should be the same, but rather that diversity of food products across the EU should be encouraged while still being subject to the same basic standards of food safety. In food-processing systems, practices in the member states which joined in 2004 have to be in line with all member states by December 2007.

Union for Europe of the Nations (UEN)   This particular grouping in the **European Parliament** is generally seen as being **eurosceptic** in nature. Outside of the **European Union** (EU), this grouping would be seen as a natural

Table U1   Parties of the Union for Europe of the Nations
              (2007)

Alleanza Nazionale (Italy)
Alleanza Siciliana (Italy)
Dansk Folkparti (Denmark)
Fianna Fáil (Ireland)
Forum Polskie (Poland)
Lega Nord per l'indipendenza della Padania (Italy)
Liberalų demokratų partija (Lithuania)
Lietuvos valstiečių liaudininkų sajunga (Lithuania)
Liga Polskich Rodzin (Poland)
Prawo i Sprawiedliwość (Poland)
Polskie Stronnictwo Ludowe (Poland)
Samoobrona RP (Poland)
Tëvzemei un Brïvïbai/LNNK (Latvia)

---

bedfellow for the **European People's Party and European Democrats** (EPP-ED). Ideologically, they are fairly similar groups. The key difference is that the EPP-ED is a pro-European grouping whereas the UEN group is far more anti-EU.

The UEN is one of the smaller groupings in the European Parliament. It has **Members of the European Parliament** from six member **state**s: Denmark, Ireland, Italy, Latvia, Lithuania and Poland. The particular political parties are listed in Table U1.

Although eurosceptic in nature, the UEN sees the opportunity to use the EU as a vehicle to push its own agenda. This includes preserving national heritages, protecting linguistic and cultural diversity, and placing a far greater emphasis upon the role of national governments rather than the EU (a form of **subsidiarity**).

United States of Europe   This is often seen as the ideal dream for **europhile**s: a single superstate, covering all of

Europe from the Ural Mountains to the Atlantic Ocean, from the Mediterranean Sea to the Arctic Ocean. All of this area would be governed by a single government, potentially modelled on the USA system of **federalism**. To **europhobes**, on the other hand, this is the nightmare scenario.

While the creation of a European superstate is still a long way off, should it ever even come to pass, the reality is that the **European Union** (EU) appears to be taking steps down such a path. As the EU acquires more areas of **competence**, including foreign and defence policy, and with the development and implementation of the single currency, speculation does indeed appear to drift towards the end goal of the European project. The problem is: what is the end goal of the EU? Is it the development of a United States of Europe? The **harmonisation** and **integration** that are currently being undertaken suggest the possibility of such an end result. Even the development of the draft **European constitution** highlights moves towards the creation of a putative **state**. Yet the defeat of the draft **constitution** at the hands of the Dutch and the French highlights a degree of resistance to such a project. Added to this, there is also resistance from national governments towards further integration. Phrases such as 'too far, too fast' have been used by **eurosceptics** for many years.

Currently, the EU has few features of a modern state. Movement to obtain more of these features is likely to be resisted by most member states. The reality is that the EU is likely to continue down the current incremental path, as envisaged by Jean **Monnet**. Some powers will be picked up, while others will be ceded to the member states. The development of a United States of Europe will require **unanimity** from all member states, and it is just not likely to happen.

V

Value Added Tax (VAT)   A tax on consumption of goods and services. It is applied to all goods and services that are bought in the **European Union**, unless the particular product is zero-rated (see below). VAT is applied at the point of purchase.

There are three rates of VAT, which indicate a degree of **harmonisation** across the EU. There is a standard rate, which is set across the EU at a minimum of 15 per cent and a maximum of 25 per cent (in the UK it is set at 17.5 per cent). There is a reduced rate, which starts at 5 per cent (which is the level set in the UK). Finally, particular goods and services may be zero-rated – for the most part, this applies to the UK and Ireland. This means that there is no VAT on these particular goods and services. Once a product has a VAT rate, it may not become zero-rated. Governments may, however, change products between the standard and reduced rates.

veto   A by-product of unanimous voting. If there is a requirement for a unanimous decision from all members of the **European Union** (for example, on the issue of **enlargement**), then this effectively gives each member **state** a **veto** over the decision.

It was the **empty chair crisis** which resulted in the **Luxembourg Compromise** that led to the idea of a national veto (or **unanimous decision-making**). Through time, and with agreements such as the **Single European Act**, the emphasis upon unanimity or national vetoes has declined. Many decisions are now taken by **Qualified Majority Voting**, although there are still specific policy areas that offer the opportunity of a veto on the grounds of national interest.

W

Werner Plan   The first plan to develop a single currency. It was detailed in 1969 in the **Werner Report** and tied all **European Economic Community** currencies to each other, as well as pegging them against the US dollar. There was a margin of fluctuation against the US dollar of +/–2.25 per cent. It was hoped that there would be a similar ceiling of divergence between the strongest and weakest European currencies. This system was known as the 'snake in the tunnel'.

Werner Report   The Werner Report led to the **Werner Plan**. It was written by Pierre Werner, prime minister of Luxembourg 1959–74 and 1979–84. The Werner Report detailed a three-stage plan towards **Economic and Monetary Union**. The exchange rates of all member states would be stabilised against each other (and pegged to the US dollar) from 1972 onwards. A single currency could then be adopted by 1980.

There are similarities between the Werner Report and the **Delors Report**. **Delors'** approach, however, did not tie the European currencies to the US dollar. Added to this, Delors also saw the necessity of transferring authority over decision-making in this area to the European institutions, rather than leaving them in national hands. In this respect, the Delors Report can be seen as being far more **supranational** in its approach when compared to the Werner Report.

Western European Union (WEU)   A defence pact that effectively replaced the **European Defence Community** in 1954. The founder members were Belgium, Britain, France, Italy, Luxembourg, the Netherlands and West Germany. At the same time, the WEU was able to facilitate West Germany's entry into the **North Atlantic Treaty Organization** (NATO) in the following year.

The WEU was overshadowed by NATO during the cold war period. Interest in the organisation was rekindled in the 1980s as a result of the limitations of **European Political Co-operation**. It must be noted, however, that the WEU was a totally separate entity from the **European Community**, although there were calls, particularly from Jacques **Delors**, for the WEU to be subsumed within the EC.

In the **Treaty on European Union** negotiations, the relationship changed. It was agreed that the WEU would provide a basis from which the **European Union** might develop some form of defence policy. The separation of the WEU and the EU has remained. Neutral countries, such as Austria, Finland, Ireland and Sweden (which are not even members of NATO and are only observers at the WEU), have expressed grave concerns about the development of a common defence policy. There is the possibility of integrating the WEU and the EU, should the **European Council** decide to adopt such an idea. Such **integration** would be likely to be subject to **unanimous decision-making**. The situation is further complicated by the fact that Iceland and Turkey, neither of which are EU member **state**s, are both members of the WEU.

WEU   see **Western European Union**

widening   Often used to describe approaches to **enlargement** of the **European Union** (EU). It tends to be presented in the form of a debate between widening and **deepening** the EU, that is, increasing the membership of the EU versus greater **integration** of the EU.

There is, however, a second usage of the term 'widening'. It can also be used to describe how the EU is taking on more tasks, or increasing the number of **competences** for which the EU is responsible. In this respect, widening the EU can be seen as part of the **supranational** aspects of the organisation.

withdrawal For a member **state** to leave the **European Union** is a very rare occurrence. Countries are clamouring to join the EU; withdrawal tends not to happen. In fact, the only example of a country leaving the EU (or more accurately, the **European Community**) is Greenland, in 1983. Norway has applied to join the EU (and its predecessors), been accepted twice but then turned down membership after a national **referendum** voted against joining on each occasion.

The draft **European constitution** included how the EU would cope with a member state deciding to withdraw. Issues such as the number of **Members of the European Parliament,** the distribution of portfolios in the **Commission** and the whole system of **qualified majority voting** in the **Council of Ministers** were all covered. Prior to such a move, the EU had not really considered the consequences of a member state deciding to quit the organisation.

X

xenophobia At its most basic level, this is the fear or even hatred of foreigners or anything foreign. It is sometimes linked to racism. Racism tends to focus upon physical differences such as skin colour. It does not, however, contain the 'phobia' or fear factor of xenophobia. Xenophobia is about behaviour based on the fact that something or someone is foreign. It could even be seen as a form of paranoia of foreign things.

Xenophobia has become more apparent with the increase in migration across the **European Union** (EU), especially with the free movement of people. Yet it can also be seen at a cultural level. In this respect, anything that does not belong to the 'home' culture or language is not just to be avoided, but to be eliminated.

There is growing concern in the EU about racism and xenophobia. The **third pillar** of the **Treaty on European Union** has, as part of its remit, the combating of xenophobia and racism.

In attempting to combat xenophobia, the European Monitoring Centre on Racism and Xenophobia was established, in 1997. On 1 March 2007, the EU replaced it with the Agency for Fundamental Rights. Finding ways to combat racism, xenophobia and related intolerance is still high on the agenda.

Y

Yaoundé Agreement   The forerunner of the **Lomé** and the **Cotonou Agreements**. Yaoundé, which is the capital of Cameroon, is where the agreement was signed, in 1963. It came into effect the following year and ran until 1970, when it was renewed as Yaoundé II. In 1975, Yaoundé was replaced by the Lomé Agreement.

The original Yaoundé Agreement was signed between the **European Economic Community** (EEC) and 18 African countries (see below), all of which were former French and Belgian colonies. It gave preferential trading status to all of the signatory **state**s. This meant greater access to the EEC market, as well as opening up their home markets to EEC products. On top of this, more economic aid was also granted to the signatory states. The original signatories of the Yaoundé Agreement were:

- Burundi
- Cameroon
- Central African Republic
- Chad
- Congo-Brazzaville
- Congo-Léopoldville
- Côte d'Ivoire
- Dahomey
- Gabon
- Madagascar
- Mali
- Mauritania
- Niger
- Rwanda
- Senegal
- Somalia
- Togo
- Upper Volta

The emphasis was very much upon the former colonies exporting industrial products to the EEC. Agricultural products, especially those in competition with European equivalents, tended to be excluded from the agreement.

Arguably, this agreement was also linked to the cold war. The European powers did not want their former colonies falling under the thrall of the Soviet Union and communism. The Yaoundé Agreement was a measure designed to prevent such things occurring.